THE
CRICKET
POCKET BIBLE

GREG VAUGHAN

PB POCKET
BIBLES

This edition first published in Great Britain 2011 by
Crimson Publishing, a division of Crimson Business Ltd
Westminster House
Kew Road
Richmond
Surrey
TW9 2ND

A catalogue record for this book is available from the British Library.

ISBN 978 1 907087 141

Printed and bound by Lego Print SpA, Trento

ACKNOWLEDGEMENTS

Many thanks to all who helped in the research and writing of this book, including Stuart at Berwyn Books, Ian for advice on umpiring and the laws, and my beloved Jenny for tea and sympathy.

CONTENTS

INTRODUCTION

What do they know of cricket, who only cricket know?
CLR James

Welcome to a wonderful world. Right from the start we've got to get something straight – cricket is not a sport. Sport is something that needs skill, training regimes and athleticism. Ok, so that's something that cricketers at the highest level need as well, but for the rest of us, the people who watch from the comfort of an arm-chair, a deckchair or a stand, even the people who spend their evenings or weekends playing the game itself, it is just that. A game.

So why is that distinction important? Well, firstly because games are typified by rules – except in cricket they're called laws – and these can be read, understood and analysed by anyone, from play-ers to spectators to officials, which makes everyone's participation very active. It's a game because anyone can play it, at any level, using even the most basic equipment. It's a game because people love it, and because it becomes part of life. It's a game because it doesn't have to matter – which is what makes it matter even more.

That's what this book celebrates; the game from root to branch, from its basics to its complexities and from its highs to its lows. You'll find all the essentials explained in these pages – from the laws of the game, to the right kind of kit, to the right way to behave on and off the field. You'll also find a full explanation of all the terms of reference and nicknames that appear like a secret code to a newcomer to the game. But most of all you'll find a wealth of information, hints, tips and background which will immediately draw you into the ranks of the cricket lover if you're not there yet. Or it will underline your passion for the game if you've already given it your heart.

This book offers more than simply guidance on how to play, it also takes a closer look at the history and playing records of the teams at the top of the game, at their star performers and their grounds, at their notorious scandals and exhilarating victories. It looks at the relationship between cricket and the world around it – in the political world, in books, on film, even in music – and at how the way we watch and play cricket is changing.

For me, cricket has been a lifelong partner – and while it hasn't been one I've had the smoothest relationship with (best bowling 4–12, best batting 20) at least I've always tried to understand and respect its ways. That's not always an easy task, but I know this book will give you a head start. So enjoy what you find in here. I hope it's the start of something beautiful. But if not, don't worry. It's only a game, after all.

Greg Vaughan

Important note: Throughout this book, the male pronoun 'he' has been used to refer to cricketers, but there is nothing in this book, nor in the laws or spirit of cricket, that does not apply equally to women as it does to men.

THE HISTORY OF CRICKET

Cricket: a sport of which the contenders drive a ball with sticks in opposition to each other.
Definition in Samuel Johnson's dictionary, published 1755

⚫ ORIGINS OF THE GAME ⚫

As the above quote shows, it's pretty hard to sum up the richly textured and much-loved game of cricket in a single, simple sentence. And as you might expect it's equally hard to pinpoint the where, when and why of the sport's genesis and transformation into the worldwide phenomenon we recognise today.

What we do have, however, is the knowledge that by the time Johnson was putting together his dictionary, cricket was a firmly established sport throughout society – and all around the world.

There are many different theories about the origins of the sport – references to bat and ball games played in medieval Holland, France and even Scandinavia all point to the existence of a form of the game in the 13th century, but there's no definitive evidence laid down until 1598, when John Derrick, a coroner from the town of Guildford in Surrey, noted in an official document that he had played cricket as a boy on a patch of land in the town as far back as the 1550s.

Stoolball – cricket's older brother?

The game of stoolball is closely linked to cricket and many people believe the two games have the same roots. But while both sports became popular in the south east UK counties of Kent, Sussex and Surrey 500 years ago, cricket has become an international sport while stoolball has remained local to that area.

The word 'stool' has nothing to do with seating – it is an old Sussex dialect word for a tree stump. Like cricket, stoolball has teams of 11 players and boundaries, runouts and fielders, but there are some differences:

- *The bat is small and round, more like a table tennis bat than a traditional cricket bat, and the ball is softer, like in baseball.*
- *The target is a wooden panel on a stake and the ball must be bowled underarm and cannot hit the ground after it is bowled.*
- *There are eight balls in an over.*

Stoolball is still widely played in Sussex and Surrey, where competitive amateur leagues keep the old game alive and well.

THE FIRST GAME: WHERE, WHEN AND WHO WON

After John Derrick there are a handful of references to cricket over the following 50 years but most of these relate to unofficial matches played on Sundays, which met with the disapproval of the church authorities and fines or penance for the unfortunate players involved. The first 'official' match on record was played at Coxheath near Maidstone in Kent on May 29 1646.

This first game was played on common land with two players on one side and four on the other. The ball was bowled underarm and the bat was a curved club, while there were only two stumps. It was a simple and unrefined game. Samuel Filmer, a noted royalist sympathiser in an era of Cromwell-inspired rebellion, was on the winning side.

THE HISTORY OF CRICKET • 3

Pocket Fact

The game at Coxheath was also notable as bets were laid on the outcome — cricket's growing popularity was closely linked to the massive increase in gambling after the restoration of the monarchy in 1660.

ORIGIN OF THE WORD 'CRICKET'

As we've already seen, cricket has a fairly sketchy history, so it's not surprising that the word itself has a range of different potential sources. Here are some of the more popular theories:

- **Krick.** Old Dutch 'a stick' or Cric, old English for 'a staff'. Both of these words relate to the bat and its shape and may be the origin of the game's title, while some histories claim that the name comes from the Dutch krickstoel, which was a low stool used for kneeling when praying in church, and which was similar in appearance to the early stumps.

- **Crekett.** This is the word used by John Derrick in the first recorded account of the game.

- **Creag.** This word relates to a game played in the court of King Edward I way back in 1299, but may just be a corruption of the Gaelic word 'craic' which was used to describe pastimes in general.

Pocket Fact

When cricket was first played on rough and uneven common land it was a pretty dangerous pastime with no pads or other protection for the batsman. The first recorded fatality on the cricket pitch was Jasper Vinall, who was hit by a bat while fielding in 1624.

THE FIRST ESTABLISHED CLUBS AND GROUNDS

As cricket became more established in the 18th century, so it became more organised and teams sprang up, leading to the creation of venues for these teams to play at. Here are some of the most important pioneering clubs and the grounds they frequented.

The clubs

- **Slindon.** A Sussex club supported by an aristocratic patron, the Duke of Richmond (1701–1750). The club attracted a number of high profile players and often represented the whole county of Sussex in games.

- **Hambledon.** If Sussex had Slindon then Hampshire trumped them with Hambledon, a team which effectively rewrote the history of the game – partly by dominating for many years and partly thanks to the stories of John Nyren, son of Hambledon legend Richard Nyren (see p. 9). Nyren's tales were recorded in *The Young Cricketer's Tutor*, a book which described the rural idyll of Hambledon in such romantic terms that it became a popular myth that cricket had been invented at Hambledon.

- **White Conduit Club (WCC).** A short-lived but vital club that emerged at the beginning of the 1780s (and ceased to exist when incorporated into the MCC in 1787) from the gentlemen's clubs of London – specifically from the Star and Garter Club which was patronised by the Prince of Wales. The team played its cricket at White Conduit Fields in London and employed a number of the leading professional cricketers of the day.

- **Marylebone Cricket Club (MCC).** The reason for the short life of the WCC was its absorption into a new club based at Dorset Square, Marylebone. Many WCC members became part of the MCC and the new club, formed in 1787, has gone on to be among the most influential in world cricket history. The MCC picked up where the Star and Garter Club left off in 1774, as the self-appointed lawmaker in the early – and fairly lawless – days of the game. Although the MCC was mainly a cricket playing club, it continued in the role of lawmaker without question or comment for almost 200 years, until the power of the game's policing body – the International Cricket Council (ICC) – grew to such an extent that the MCC now fills a role as keeper and publisher of the laws rather than the actual enforcer. See Chapter 2 for more on the MCC, its role as cricket's first real law enforcement body, and its relationship with the ICC.

- **Calcutta Cricket Club.** English ex-pats had formed the CCC in India by 1792. The club is still in existence and is one of the oldest sporting clubs in the world.

Pocket Fact

As mentioned above in the case of Slindon, the earliest games had a county versus county focus, which is believed to be the main inspiration behind the English format of county teams rather than town or city based teams.

The grounds

- **Artillery Ground.** An existing ground in Finsbury in north London which was often used for first-class games from the 1730s to the 1770s.

- **Moulsey Hurst.** West Molesey, Surrey. Another of the great early grounds and the setting for the painting *Cricket at Moulsey Hurst* which hangs at Lord's. The first recorded match to be played there took place in 1726.

- **Broadhalfpenny Down.** The home of Hambledon Cricket Club in Hambledon village in Hampshire.

- **Bishopbourne Paddock.** The ground at Bourne House near Canterbury, Kent, owned by one of the game's early patrons, Sir Horace Mann. Many professional games were played here in the latter half of the 18th century.

- **Lord's.** The home of the MCC and the cradle of all cricket. Its origins are not so romantic – it was founded by cricketer and property speculator Thomas Lord, who had operated several grounds in London before settling on a site at St John's Wood in London in 1814. Lord hoped to develop for profit, building houses around the ground but the plan never came to fruition and while Lord faded into the background his name stuck.

● DEVELOPMENT OF THE GAME ● AND ITS LAWS

With the game taking on legitimacy in society and with clubs and grounds set in stone, it became vital for the game to further develop its own laws and regulations. Here's a brief outline of some of cricket's major milestones.

1727: The Duke of Richmond and a Mr Brodrick establish articles of agreement before a match – the first written 'laws' of the game.

1744: The London Club (based at the Artillery Ground) produces the first version of the laws of cricket, establishing certain key rules, including the set length of a pitch as 22 yards.

Pocket Fact

In the early 1770s, a Surrey-based player Thomas White came out to the crease carrying a bat as wide as the stumps. The furore from this incident led to a regulation size for bats which continues to this day.

1771: Bat width is set at four and a quarter inches.

1774: The law of leg before wicket (lbw) is introduced.

1775: The middle stump is added.

Pocket Fact

John Small of Hambledon survived against the great bowler 'Lumpy' Stevens (see p. 10) after the ball passed between the two stumps on numerous occasions. A third stump was soon added and another loophole was closed.

1787: The MCC is formed.

1788: The MCC issues a revised version of the laws of cricket.

1804: The first official reference to cricket being played in Australia.

1828: Round-arm bowling (in which the player's hand is level with his elbow) is finally permitted by the MCC following a 20-year struggle to have it recognised.

The great bowling debate

When cricket first became popular, the ball was rolled underarm along the ground. The quality of cricket fields made this dangerous for the batsman and erratic for the bowler. It soon became clear that bowlers could be more effective if they pitched the ball through the air, as the extra 'flight' would make the ball move or behave in a less predictable way.

In 1807, John Willes pioneered a new form of bowling in which the hand was level with the elbow and the ball was delivered in a round-arm action. It was regarded as dangerous – as the ball could be released at much greater speed – and was eventually banned by the MCC in 1816. However, Willes continued to bowl in this way, and won many supporters to his cause. After a series of campaigns by high-profile players, who could see the improvements round-arm bowling was making to their game, the MCC's nerve finally broke in 1828 and round-arm bowling was accepted. By the time overarm bowling was accepted in 1864,

> *the traditionalists had lost some of their influence and the*
> *transition was smoother – although round-arm and overarm*
> *techniques were both used right up to the end of the*
> *19th century, with WG Grace (see p. 11) a particularly*
> *great exponent of the round-arm delivery.*

1830s: Pads are introduced for batsmen.

1832: First official reference to cricket being played in New Zealand.

1844: The first international match takes place – between Canada and the USA.

1846: All-England XI founded.

1850: Wicketkeeping gloves are introduced.

1864: MCC approves overarm bowling.

1877: Australia play England in the first test match. Australia win by 45 runs.

1889: South Africa play their first test match.

1900: The number of balls per over is changed from five to six.

1910: The definition of a 'six' is changed to any hit over the boundary that does not touch the ground.

1928: West Indies play their first test match.

1930: New Zealand play their first test match.

1931: Stumps are widened and heightened by one inch (to 28 inches and nine inches respectively).

1932: India play their first test match.

1948: The length of test matches is set at five days.

1952: Pakistan play their first test match.

1963: The first one-day tournament in cricket – the Gillette Cup – is launched in England.

1969: One-day Sunday league cricket begins in England.

1970: South Africa is banned from international cricket due to the government's apartheid policy.

1971: The first one-day international takes place. Australia beat England by five wickets.

1975: The first limited overs World Cup takes place. West Indies beat Australia in the final.

1978: First time a helmet is worn in a test match – by Graham Yallop of Australia.

1982: Sri Lanka play their first test match.

1991: South Africa are readmitted to international cricket.

1992: Zimbabwe play their first test match.

1993: The MCC splits from the ICC (International Cricket Council).

2000: Bangladesh play their first test match.

2000: The laws of cricket are revised.

2003: Twenty20 Cup launched in England.

2007: First Twenty20 World Cup held in South Africa.

2008: Indian Premier League – the world's richest cricket tournament – begins.

● EARLY PIONEERS ●

Great clubs, great grounds and an ever-growing list of laws and regulations didn't make the game great alone – that honour fell to a select band of pioneers who, in various ways, took the game to a new level of skill and professionalism. Here are some of the key players in the earlier days of the game.

Richard Nyren (1734–1797)

- **His claim to fame:** One of the leading players of Hambledon, the club which dominated cricket for so long in the 18th century. Nyren was less noted for his cricket than for his ability to spot talent and nurture his team. He also ran the celebrated Bat and Ball pub in the village.

- **Legendary status:** 9/10. Assured of his place in cricketing literature as the the main character of his son John's bestselling book *The Young Cricketer's Tutor* (see p. 4).

Edward 'Lumpy' Stevens (1735–1819)

- **His claim to fame:** The finest bowler of underarm 'shooters' – a fast, almost unplayable ball that pitched perfectly nearly every time – Stevens was also one of the earliest examples of a professional player. Employed by his patron notionally as a gardener but mainly as a demon bowler, Lumpy played the game well into his fifties.

- **Legendary status:** 7/10. His portrait hangs at Knole House in Kent and his employer commissioned a gravestone on his death – not bad for a simple working man.

William Clarke (1798–1856)

- **His claim to fame:** He was a bowler of great ability, but his major feat was to assemble an All-England XI, effectively the first incarnation of any national cricket team anywhere in the world. He also created the famous Trent Bridge cricket ground.

- **Legendary status:** 8/10. A wily businessman, Clarke was a true visionary who saw the potential for the game as a spectator sport.

Fuller Pilch (1804–1870)

- **His claim to fame:** What Lumpy Stevens did for bowling, Pilch emulated with the bat. Pilch totally dominated the game from 1830–1850 and was the finest batsman in England by a huge margin. He introduced the idea of playing on the front foot, a great advantage on the uneven pitches of the era. He scored 10 centuries in his first class playing career at a time when high scores were almost impossible on rough pitches.

- **Legendary status:** 9/10. A pioneer, whose supreme batting ability overcame the limitations of the poor quality early pitches.

John Wisden (1826–1884)

- **His claim to fame:** Wisden was part of Clarke's XI for a time and is notable for the extraordinary achievement of taking all 10 wickets in an innings for North v South England. But his principal claim lies in his extraordinary records of the scores, averages and records of cricket, which continue to this day in the shape of *Wisden's Cricket Almanack* – otherwise known as 'the bible' (see Chapter 10).

- **Legendary status:** 10/10. Alongside Thomas Lord, Wisden is a name that will forever be associated with the game of cricket.

WG Grace (1848–1915)

- **His claim to fame:** Grace was the first superstar cricketer. A larger-than-life character, he was simply a better player than anyone who came before – especially with the bat. But Grace was also a great showman who had the capacity to command huge crowds (and huge fees) when he played. The fact that he turned cricket into a commercial success as a player – rather than simply as a betting supporter – helped to bring the game's standards into the 20th century. Cricket grounds began to resemble their modern-day equivalents because of the money that followed in Grace's wake.

- **Legendary status.** 10/10. An icon of the game. With more than 54,000 career runs to his name and nearly 3,000 wickets, he was much more than a mere circus act.

Pocket Fact 🏏

England suffered a 45-run defeat in the first ever test match (against Australia in 1877) and when the fixture was repeated exactly 100 years later England lost again, by exactly the same margin.

2

THE LAWS OF CRICKET

Cricket is a game full of forlorn hopes and sudden dramatic changes of fortune, and its rules are so ill-defined that their interpretation is partly an ethical business.
George Orwell

● A GAME OF LAWS NOT RULES ●

Knowing that cricket is a game governed by laws rather than rules gives us an insight into the seriousness and the complexity of the game's regulations – it exists within a world of its own, as Orwell explained. This allows us to see how open the laws can be to interpretation or, potentially, abuse (see Chapter 9 for some of the game's worst excesses). But it also explains why the laws and the upholders of the laws rely so heavily on every participant sticking to the 'spirit' of the game.

ORIGINS OF THE LAWS

The lawmakers

As we've already seen, when the MCC was originally established in 1787 by some of the leading players and patrons of English cricket, it took it upon itself to establish a clear structure and to develop laws for the burgeoning game. The MCC has continued to play a part in lawmaking, although it is now the publisher of the laws rather than the enforcer – it is the International Cricket Council (ICC) which is responsible for enforcing laws and punishing breaches in the international game (see p. 15), while each nation deals with internal cricket issues through a governing body that is separate from the ICC – for example the England and Wales Cricket Board (ECB) in the UK.

Although the MCC is accepted as the authority for publishing and maintaining cricket's laws around the world, the first attempt to draft laws for the game took place almost 50 years before the MCC was formed, in 1744. The gentlemen and noblemen of the London Club, based at the Artillery Ground, drew up the earliest recorded code, although there's no indication that this was anything other than the rules governing a particular match.

Early laws

Some of the earliest laws drawn up by the London Club that are still in existence include:

- Restrictions on the weight of the ball (but not yet of its size).
- A regulation height of the stumps.
- Dimensions of the cricket pitch.
- The need for a coin toss to start the game.
- A 'no ball' rule.
- Ways of getting out (such as obstructing fielders and hitting the ball twice).

This code was revised by members of the Star and Garter Club (see p. 4) in 1755 and then again in 1774. It was further updated by a collection of players from Kent, Hampshire, Surrey, Sussex, Middlesex and London in 1786. The first code of laws to be produced by the MCC was approved in May 1788. The code has been continually revised and updated through the years, with new versions being published in 1835, 1884, 1947, 1979, 1992 and 2000.

The MCC today

The influence of the MCC around the world is largely based on its reputation as the oldest surviving professional club, as all changes to the laws are now made in close consultation with national and international cricket authorities. The MCC holds the copyright on the Laws of Cricket, which have now been around for 250 years and have served the game pretty well even though times have changed. The most recent code of laws, issued in 2000, included a preamble defining the Spirit of Cricket – which emphasises the need for honesty in the players and the responsibility of their captains to uphold this spirit.

The spirit of the game

'Cricket is a game that owes much of its unique appeal to the fact that it should be played not only within its laws but also within the spirit of the game. Any action which is seen to abuse the spirit causes injury to the game itself.'

The Spirit of Cricket, MCC.

This preamble explains that the captains of each team are responsible for the actions and behaviour of their players. It specifies the ultimate responsibility of the umpires in determining fair and unfair play. Above all though it explains that all of the players share responsibility for ensuring the game is played with respect for officials, team-mates and opponents. It has been invoked in many recent scandals and questions of etiquette (see Chapters 5 and 9 for more on this).

ICC (International Cricket Council)

The ICC was originally established – as the Imperial Cricket Conference – by representatives from England, South Africa and Australia in 1909 as a way of collectively managing the growing international game. Until 1993, it was allied to the MCC and was based at Lord's, so the two organisations worked in close partnership. The ICC was intended to be responsible for administration of the day-to-day business of organising cricket matches between countries, planning international tournaments and dealing with breaches of discipline on the international stage.

The ICC became a separate organisation in 1993 so it could have a truly independent view of world cricket, without any ties to a particular test nation. It is now the world governing body of cricket and is responsible not just for international cricket but for the promotion and continued growth of cricket as a game in around 100 nations. Since 2005, the ICC has underlined its independence from the MCC by basing itself in Dubai. The ICC also conducts investigations into match-fixing, investigates and trials new technology and continues to work with the MCC and with national governing bodies throughout the world to develop the game.

🏏 THE ESSENTIALS OF THE GAME 🏏

On a basic level the game involves two teams with the simple objective of scoring more runs than each other or bowling out all the batsmen in the opposing team before they reach their target. The order of play is determined when the captains of the teams toss a coin on the wicket – the playing area in the centre of the field of play – and the winner of the toss then decides whether to bat – sending in the first two batsmen to begin the team's innings – or to field. The fielding captain has nine fielders to position (see fielding positions p. 30) as well as a bowler and wicketkeeper. Games of all lengths and forms begin in this fashion.

Essential glossary

Here's an overview of some of the key terms we'll be discussing in this chapter (for a full glossary of terms see Chapter 11).

- **Bails.** *The bails are the two small cylindrical pieces of wood that sit across the top of the three stumps to make the wicket which the batsman defends. If the stumps are hit the bails must be dislodged for the batsman to be declared out.*
- **Boundary.** *The perimeter of the playing area, marked in white.*
- **Bye.** *A run that is added to the batting team's total but that doesn't come off the bat. Leg byes are runs scored off the pads. Byes are not counted against the bowler.*
- **Crease.** *The area that the batsman occupies in front of the wicket.*

- **Innings.** *An innings is the turn of each team to bat. One-day games are single innings matches, games played over two or more days will allow each team two innings.*
- **Over.** *A set of six deliveries bowled from one end of the pitch. At the end of each over, the play switches to the opposite end of the pitch and a different bowler begins another over. An extra ball must be bowled in an over for any deliveries that are unlawful (no-ball or wide).*
- **Pitch.** *The 22-yard playing surface in the centre of the ground with stumps at either end. Also called a wicket.*
- **Stumps.** *The three cylindrical wooden stakes at either end of the pitch which are topped by bails.*
- **Wicket.** *See pitch.*

● THE LAWS OF THE GAME ● EXPLAINED

There are 42 laws in the current code of cricket and they relate equally to players of either gender. Some are highly technical and specific and need no more than a brief mention, while some need a more detailed explanation. The laws can be broken down into the following broad areas:

- **Laws 1–4:** The participants in the game, players, umpires and scorers.

- **Laws 5–11:** The equipment and the playing area, including size and weight of bats and balls, and dimensions of pitch.

- **Laws 12–17:** The structure and length of the game, intervals, beginning and end of play.

- **Laws 18–29:** Scoring methods, including runs scored off the bat and penalty runs.

- **Laws 30–39:** The 10 ways in which a batsman can be dismissed.

- **Laws 40–42:** Permitted equipment for fielding and responsibilities of the captain relating to fair and unfair play. These laws also cover special conditions.

LAWS 1–4: THE PARTICIPANTS

- **Players and substitutes.** Matches are usually played by two teams of 11 players. It is possible to play the game with fewer or more players, but only 11 may field at any one time. Substitutes may stand in for an injured or ill player but they may not bat, bowl or play as wicketkeeper (see p. 168 for more on substitutes and runners).

- **Umpires and scorers.** There are two umpires and two scorers for each match. The umpires make sure the field of play is correctly laid out and that all equipment is standard. They are also the judges of fair play. One umpire stands at the bowler's end of the pitch and the other usually stands square of the wicket near the fielding position of square leg (see fielding positions p. 30).

LAWS 5–11: THE EQUIPMENT AND PLAYING AREA

- **The ball.** A regulation cricket ball weighs no less than five and a half ounces (155.9g) and no more than five and three-quarter ounces (163g). It should have a diameter just short of nine inches (22.9cm).

- **The bat.** A bat is made up of two parts – a handle and a blade, both of which should be made from wood. While the width of the bat is fixed (see Chapter 1 for history), the height and weight of the bat are determined more by the batsman's requirements, size and style – though the height for a bat is restricted to a maximum of 38in (97cm). Most bats for adults weigh about a kilo, and use of a lighter bat is generally acknowledged to be a good way of improving technique and all-round batting style.

Pocket Fact

If a bowled ball hits any part of the batsman's glove while it is in contact with the bat and is then caught by a fielder then the batsman can be given out.

- **Size of playing area.** While the overall size of the field of play is not determined by law, the size of the pitch – the rectangular strip bracketed at either end by three stumps topped by bails – is fixed. Pitches are 22 yards (20.12m) long and 10ft (3.05m) wide. The wickets (stumps and bails) are nine inches (22.86cm) wide and 28 inches (71.1cm) high.

- **The batting crease.** The wickets are at the rear of a rectangular area marked with white lines and known as a crease. The line running through the stumps is the bowling crease, the line parallel with this 4ft (1.22m) in front of it is the popping crease and the lines which bisect these and complete the 'sides' of the rectangle are known as the return crease. When the batsman (or just the bat) is touching the ground inside this crease he cannot be given out stumped or run out (see p. 22).

LAWS 12–17: THE STRUCTURE OF THE GAME

These laws relate to the number of innings in a game. If it is a match of two innings per side then there are conditions governing declarations (where a team's captain declares the innings closed even if all the batsmen aren't yet out) and follow-on (when a team has not made sufficient runs in their reply to a first innings and must bat again – the total needed to avoid the 'follow-on' varies depending on the form of cricket being played).

These laws are also concerned with the length of sessions of play and length of intervals.

LAWS 18–29: SCORING

The objective in cricket is to score more runs than the other team. A run can be scored in a variety of ways:

- **Running between the wickets.** The captain of the fielding team nominates a bowler to bowl from each end of the pitch. The bowlers bowl six balls in an over, unless any of the balls are illegal (see below), in which case more balls must be bowled. If the batsman hits the ball and the two batsmen cross, running the length of the pitch from one crease to the other, a run is scored. The batsmen can continue to run until the ball is returned to the wicket by a fielder, meaning the potential runs from each delivery are unlimited, but in reality the maximum all-run score is four as no ground is so large (and no batsman so quick) that more runs can be taken.

- **Overthrows.** If a member of the fielding side throws the ball back to the wicket but it isn't properly gathered and runs away into the outfield the batsmen may run 'overthrows' until the ball is returned to the wicket. If the throw from the fielder is completely missed at the wicket and it runs all the way over the boundary it is given as four overthrows and is added to whatever score the batsman took from that ball. Hence, it is theoretically possible to score eight from one ball – four all-run singles plus four overthrows.

- **Boundaries.** The boundary marks the limit of the field of play. It is sometimes marked with rope and sometimes with a white line. If the batsman hits the ball over this boundary without the ball first hitting the ground on the field of play, six runs are scored. If the ball hits the field of play before crossing the boundary, four runs are scored.

- **No-balls.** A no-ball is indicated by the umpire when the bowler's front foot is completely beyond the popping crease when the ball is released. Other reasons for calling a no-ball include the throwing of the ball by the bowler, if the ball is bowled from wider than the return crease or if the fielding team is breaking field restrictions (see limited over cricket rules p. 80). The penalty for a no-ball is one run to the batting team, plus whatever runs were scored from the ball, plus an extra ball to be bowled in the over. If a batsman is caught or bowled by a no-ball the dismissal is void.

- **Wide balls.** A wide ball is called by the umpire if the bowled ball passes so wide of the batsman that it could not be reached using a normal cricket stroke. The penalty is one run – or more if the batsmen run or if the ball reaches the boundary. An extra ball must be bowled in the over.

- **Byes and leg byes.** A bye is scored when the batsman doesn't make contact with the delivery but is able to run subsequently – normally after a fielding error behind the wicket. Byes are runs that are added to the total score but don't get added to the batsman's total or marked down against the bowler's total. These are known as extras, and are marked separately in the scorebook (see scoring p. 24). Leg byes are runs scored when the batsman plays a shot but only his pad or body connects with the ball. They are added to the score in the same way as byes.

- **Penalty runs.** These are given to the batting team if anyone on the fielding side uses anything apart from his own body to stop the ball. That would include using a hat or helmet to stop or catch a ball. They can also be added to the fielding side's total if the batting side are thought by the umpires to be wasting time or damaging the pitch deliberately. Five runs are awarded for a penalty.

Pocket Fact ✏

Kent's county ground at Canterbury was distinctive among professional cricket grounds as being the only one with a tree on the field of play. The lime tree that grew on the boundary's edge was a famous landmark for many years. If a ball hit the tree, four runs were awarded to the batsman. The tree – believed to be more than 200 years old – sadly blew down in strong gales in 2005.

LAWS 30–39: GETTING OUT

There are 10 ways a batsman can lose his wicket. Most of these will require an appeal from the fielding side – a cry of 'How's that?' – before the umpire is obliged to offer a decision. The batsman is not obliged to leave the field unless he is given out by the umpire (though this practice of 'walking' is often believed to be a sign of good etiquette – see p. 67).

1. **Caught.** If a bowled ball hits the bat or gloves of a batsman and is then caught by a member of the fielding side, including the bowler, the batsman is out. In the event of a batsman being caught behind the wicket, an appeal may be required if the batsman doesn't 'walk' to indicate he has hit the ball.

2. **LBW (leg before wicket).** If a ball is bowled in such a way that it hits (or would hit) the pitch in line with the wickets and would then go on to hit the wicket, but strikes the batsman on the leg or body instead, the umpire may decide the ball would have hit the wicket and will give him out if the fielding side appeal.

3. **Bowled.** If a bowled ball hits the wicket of the batsman and dislodges a bail, the batsman is out bowled, even if the ball has hit the bat or some part of the body first. No appeal is required.

4. **Stumped.** If the batsman moves his body and bat outside the popping crease attempting to play a shot and misses the ball, the wicketkeeper can dislodge the bails with the ball and stump the batsman.

5. **Hit wicket.** If the batsman steps backwards and breaks the wicket while attempting to play a shot he is given out. As in all of the above cases, the wicket is awarded to the bowler.

6. **Run out.** If batsmen are attempting a run and the ball is thrown to either wicket and they cannot get their bat or any part of their body into the popping crease, they can be run out by a member of the fielding side dislodging the bails of that wicket.

7. **Handled ball.** If a batsman deliberately handles the ball to stop it hitting the wicket he is out.

8. **Hit ball twice.** If a batsman deliberately hits any delivery twice, he is given out.

9. **Obstructing a fielder.** If a batsman stands in the way of any member of the fielding side he can be given out by the umpire.

10. **Timed out.** If a wicket falls, the next batsman must be in position and ready to face the next ball within three minutes or he will be given out by the umpire. In practice, this dismissal has never occurred in the first-class game.

LAWS 40–42

Special conditions

There are many conditions and variations to the laws of cricket that depend on the form of the game that's being played. More information on the variations that apply in limited over cricket and in other forms are given in detail in Chapter 6. These variations are normally called rules to differentiate them from the game's fundamental laws.

Pocket Fact

If you've tried explaining the laws to a novice and they're still unsure, give them this simple and much-loved guide to the game: You have two sides, one out in the field and one in. Each man that's in the side that's in goes out and when he's out the next man goes in until he's out. When the men who were in are all out, the team who are out go in and the team who were in go out and try to get the others out. Simple.

Back when cricket was the pastime of the labourer, the score was kept by marking notches on a stick. Thankfully, the game has moved on apace since then and modern scorebooks are complex records which provide the basis for the extraordinary level of statistical analysis that underlies so many cricket lovers' fascination with the game.

⬤ THE SCOREBOOK AND SCORING ⬤

	Batsman	Time/Over In/Out		Minutes Balls	Innings of: **World Greats XI**		How Out	Bowler	Total
1	HOBBS J	11.00 1			3 - 4 - 4 - 1				
2	RICHARDS B	11.00 1	11.10 3	10	2 \\\\ //		BOWLED	MCGRATH	2
3	BRADMAN D	11.11 3			6 - 6 - 4				
4	TENDULKAR S								
5	RICHARDS V								
6	SOBERS G								
7	AKRAM W								
8	KNOTT A								
9	HADLEE R								
10	WARNE S								
11	MURALITHARAN M								

Fall of Wicket	1	2	3	4	5	6	7	8	9	10		Fielding	bye I			
Score	7											Extras	leg bye II		Sub Total	
												Bowling	wides II			
												Extras	no balls I		Extras	
												Penalty	prev innings			
												Penalty	this innings		Total	

Bowler	Bowling Analysis										Totals		Balls	Overs	Mons	Runs	Wkts	Ave
	1	2	3	4	5	6	7	8	9	10	WB	NB						
MCGRATH G	• • • • • M	2 + W • • • •	△ ▽ • • • 6															
	0-0	3-1	9-1															
BOTHAM I	1 • o • • • • •	▽ + • 4 • • • 4	╳															
	4-0	13-0																
KUMBLE A	1 • 4 6 4 •																	
	12-0																	

2	=	Runs	W = Wicket	⊙⊙	=	No Ball & Byes
△	=	Byes	● = Dot Ball (No Run)	+	=	Wide Ball
▽	=	Leg Byes	o = No Ball	⊹	=	Wide Ball & Byes
M	=	Maiden	② = No Ball & Runs			

Pocket Fact

Professional (and wealthy amateur) scorers have abandoned the notebook for the netbook — laptop computers and sophisticated computer programs are commonplace among serious scorers in the modern game.

A typical scorecard for an innings of a game will list all 11 batsmen in order, with the first batsman to receive a ball in first place. Every ball a batsman receives — even non-scoring balls known as 'dot' balls — gets marked against his name and a corresponding mark is made further down the page against each bowler's name.

If a run is scored this is marked to the credit of batsman and debit of bowler and a run is added to the total, marked off on a tally — usually on the right hand side of the page. The scorer records all wide balls and no-balls against the bowler and in the extras column and all leg byes and byes in the extras column only.

The scorers also mark the fall of wickets and note a 'maiden' over — that is one in which no runs are scored by the batsmen or debited to the bowler as penalty runs. Statistics play a massive part in the post-game discussions, so it's standard practice to have two scorers, one representing each side, in a competitive match.

THE DUCKWORTH–LEWIS METHOD

The Duckworth–Lewis (D–L) method is a way to determine the target for the team batting second in a weather-affected limited overs game. It was devised by British statisticians Frank Duckworth and Tony Lewis and is designed to be a fair way of calculating a total based on the normal conditions of play. It was first used in 1996–1997 for the one-day series between England and Zimbabwe, before being adopted by the ICC in 2001.

Prior to the D–L method, limited overs games that were affected by the weather saw the team batting second have their target reduced using a variety of methods, none of which represented a fair assessment of the game. The advantage of the D–L method is that it analyses the 'resources' used by each team when a break occurs – these resources being the number of overs that remain and the number of wickets in hand.

The best way to illustrate the method's logic is with an example. When England played India in a one day international in 2008, India's innings was interrupted by rain and the decision was taken to reduce the contest to a game of 22 overs per side. India had made a total of 166 for 4. Using the D–L method, a revised target was calculated for England based on the same number of overs. The target was 198, higher than that posted by India because it allowed for the fact that India would have scored at a higher rate if they had known the innings was just 22 overs long. The team batting first is normally expected to score heavily in their final few overs, especially if they have a lot of wickets remaining – and this potential is taken into account when the target is adjusted. England scored 178 for 8 from their 22 overs, meaning India had won the game by 19 runs using the D–L method.

Methods of calculation

The match referee will calculate the revised target. At the highest level this is always done with reference to a specially-devised computer program. Lower down the levels, tables of resource percentages are available to help the calculations. Either way round, it's a complex business.

Pocket Fact

Tony Lewis and Frank Duckworth were appointed MBEs (Members of the Order of the British Empire) in 2010. In the same year, the iconic pair gained further credibility when 'The Duckworth–Lewis Method' was used as the name of a band created by musicians Neil Hannon, of The Divine Comedy, and Tom Walsh for a cricket concept album.

● UMPIRES ●

The umpire's job is not always a happy one, but it is central to the game. As we've seen above, the two umpires in a game are the ultimate arbiters of fair play. They also have a dizzying array of responsibilities and must possess exceptional eyesight and an encyclopaedic knowledge of the game. Some of the key duties involved in being an umpire include:

- Meeting the captains and scorers prior to the game.

- Overseeing the toss of the coin.

- Inspecting the playing area prior to the start of the game to ensure it is prepared within the laws and safe for use.

- Helping batsmen to 'take their guard'. When a batsman begins his innings, he takes guard by marking a position in line with the stumps using the toe end of his bat which enables him to know where he is standing in relation to the stumps behind him. Batsmen typically take their guard in a line from middle stump, leg stump (the stump nearest their legs) or from a space between the two (middle and leg).

- Counting all balls delivered – whether they are standing at the bowler's end or not.

- Receiving and responding to appeals from the fielding side.

- Signalling decisions and scoring deliveries to the scorers and crowd.

- Monitoring the batsman's runs in case one is run short (ie without touching the ground inside the crease).

- Monitoring and deciding on light conditions and, ultimately, deciding when to stop play for bad light or rain interruption.

- Dealing with breaches of discipline, especially by the fielding side, by consulting with the captain and players involved.

The umpire's signals

- **Out.** If a batsman is adjudged to be out following an appeal from the fielding side the umpire raises an index finger above his head.
- **Wide.** Marked by extending both arms horizontally.
- **No-ball.** Marked by extending one arm horizontally.
- **Four.** A boundary four is marked by waving an arm from side to side across the chest.
- **Six.** A boundary six is marked by raising both arms above the head.
- **Bye.** Marked by raising one arm above head.
- **Leg bye.** One leg is raised and tapped by hand.
- **Short run.** One hand tapped on shoulder.
- **Dead ball.** When the ball runs away but no run is possible, or when a bowler stops before delivering the ball, a dead ball is indicated by waving both hands in a criss-cross across the waist.
- **Ignore last signal.** When a mistaken signal has been given, the umpire revokes the signal by touching both shoulders with the opposite hand.
- **New ball taken.** In the long form of the game, a new ball can be taken by the fielding side after 80 overs. The umpire holds the ball aloft to signal this.

THE THIRD UMPIRE

In international cricket, it has become commonplace for certain decisions to be referred to a third umpire, who has the benefit of television technology and can help the umpires determine certain debatable decisions such as:

- Whether a batsman has been run out or stumped by a member of the fielding side.

- Whether a ball has carried to the hands of a fielder claiming a catch.

- Whether a fielder has prevented a ball going for four or six over the boundary.

Tom Smith, the umpire's umpire.

If the statisticians have the Wisden Cricketers' Almanack *as their official bible, so the name of Tom Smith is hallowed in umpiring circles. It was Smith who for many years edited the book that now bears his name as a lasting tribute –* Tom Smith's Cricket Umpiring and Scoring. *Smith was originally a football referee who founded the Association of Cricket Umpires and Scorers (ACU&S), which has now become part of the England and Wales Cricket Board Association of Cricket Officials, the body which gives support and guidance to all who officiate at cricket matches.*

🏏 CAPTAINCY 🏏

The captain's role extends far beyond just deciding where to place fielders, although this is a core skill. From providing the motivation and discipline within the team to playing a key tactical role, the modern captain needs to be part general, part philosopher. The role's other key responsibilities include:

- **Selecting the team and deciding on batting order.** This is based on fitness, team strategy and the strength of the opposition.

- **Making the right call after winning the toss.** This skill is based on an understanding of pitch conditions, local weather conditions and the relative strengths of the teams.

- **Rotating the bowlers.** Knowing when to use and when to rest certain bowlers is a key part of the man-management role of the captain. In limited overs cricket this is partly an exercise in mathematics – making sure you have allowed for your attack bowlers to use their full allowance of overs (maximum of 10 overs per bowler in a 50-over game).

- **Making the right calls on declarations and the follow-on.** In the longer form of the game, the captain of a team which is building a big total must be able to judge the right time to declare that innings closed and exert maximum pressure on the opponents. Equally, a captain whose side has dismissed their opponents for fewer runs than are required to make his team bat again, must decide whether to make the opponents begin their second innings – or follow-on. The wrong call could take the initiative away from his team at a stroke.

- **Setting an example**. It might seem obvious, but the pressure to set a good example with bat or ball to team mates has undermined the confidence of many great players who have failed to become great captains – the likes of Kevin Pietersen, Ian Botham, Shahid Afridi and Brian Lara all suffered terrible loss of form when faced with the task of leading their country.

● THE TEAMS ●

FIELDING POSITIONS

As we've already seen, the fielding team cannot have any more than 11 players on the field of play at any one time. The nominated 'opening' bowler marks his run-up to the wicket and the wicketkeeper (wearing special webbed wicketkeeping gloves and short pads) stands behind the facing batsman's wicket.

The captain then places the remaining fielders in positions that suit the style and pace of the bowler – and take into account any failings of the batsman. The field is split into two sides, the off side is the side the batsman faces, the leg (or on) side is the side behind him. For a right-handed batsman the standard field placing would be as follows (from the off side, anti-clockwise).

FIELDING POSITIONS
(RIGHT HANDED BATSMAN)

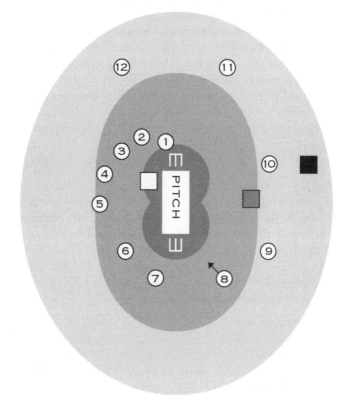

1	=	Wicketkeeper	9	=	Mid Wicket
2	=	Slip(s)	10	=	Square Leg
3	=	Gully	11	=	Fine Leg
4	=	Point	12	=	Third Man
5	=	Cover	☐	=	Silly (Point/Leg etc)
6	=	Extra Cover	▥	=	Short (Leg/Mid On etc)
7	=	Mid Off	◼	=	Deep (Midwicket/Square Leg etc)
8	=	Mid On			

Wicketkeeper

The only fielder permitted to wear protective gloves, the wicket-keeper catches the deliveries that the batsman doesn't hit as well as being the main catching fielder. His position is slightly to the left of a right-handed batsman's wicket so that he has a clear sight of the bowler's approach. His distance from the wicket depends on the speed of the bowler. For a spinner or slow swing bowler the wicketkeeper may stand very close to the wicket (as the ball won't travel fast off the pitch and it improves his chances of a stumping if the batsman leaves his crease). For a fast bowler, the wicket-keeper will stand much further back. Great wicketkeepers, like Alan Knott of England and Adam Gilchrist of Australia, are also great athletes, as keeping wicket is a very mentally-demanding job.

Slips

This is a position to the side of the wicketkeeper and heavily used by fast bowlers for behind-the-wicket catches. There can be up to four slips – and great fast bowlers like Glenn McGrath of Australia or Malcolm Marshall of the West Indies would often use a full slip cordon. Great slip fielders include Andrew Flintoff, Paul Collingwood and Ian Botham of England, Mark Waugh and Ian Chappell of Australia and Chris Gayle of the West Indies.

Third man/fly slip

Third man is an outfield position designed to save boundaries or to take catches in the deep. In reality, not many catches find their way to third man, but wayward drives (see section on batting, p. 46) can often clear the slips, meaning third man is a useful run-saving position. Fly slip is deep slip, halfway between slip and third man.

Gully

A position that is still behind the bat, but wide of the slips. It helps to be a good catcher of the ball at gully as this is often the position where the ball comes hardest, cut or driven by the batsman.

Point

This area is square of the stumps and often about one-third of the way to the boundary. It can be a popular position for the captain to occupy as it allows a good view of the action. Australia's Steve Waugh was a notable point fielder.

Covers (including extra cover and cover point)

This is the area from the midpoint of the pitch to the facing wicket from the batsman's perspective. It's a big area and the most athletic cricketers thrive in it – like England's James Anderson and Derek Randall or South Africa's Jonty Rhodes.

Mid off/on

Another popular position for captains because of the good view it affords, the mid off, and on side equivalent mid on, support the bowler and cut off straight driven shots. Deeper positions known as long off/on are used when a batsman is driving a lot of balls straight.

Midwicket

This is the mirror position for the covers, and involves an equal degree of athleticism.

Square leg

A position opposite point, normally the resting ground of the umpire not standing at the wicket.

Fine leg/leg slip

Fine leg is a position usually occupied by the bowler who is not in action. If fast bowlers are working in tandem there can be a lot of action at fine leg as glances and hooks often go off the batsman's legs and run very fine to this area. Leg slip, like fly slip, is an infield position often used to limit a batsman's scoring rate.

Close catching positions

A range of positions around the bat can be used to pressurise the batsman. These are especially useful when a fast bowler is trying to get a less confident batsman out, or when a spin bowler is getting a lot of turn (see section on bowling, p. 47). These positions reflect other fielding positions but are prefixed by the word 'short' or 'silly' to indicate the peril of standing so close to the bat – silly point, silly mid on etc. Protective clothing is often worn. England's Ian Bell and Alastair Cook have enjoyed great success in the position of short leg.

Pocket Fact

When a fielding team wants to attack or intimidate the batsman — if he's just come in or isn't very confident — the fielders gather around the bat in close positions. If it is late in the day, the fielders cast shadows across the pitch. They mustn't move until the batsman has played the ball though so that they don't distract him — otherwise a no-ball is given.

THE BATTING TEAM

Before a team begin their innings, the batting order is supplied by the captain or a team official to the scorers, so that scorecards can be drawn up. This order rarely changes in the course of an innings, but it is not set in stone, so any player can — in theory — bat in any position. The different batting positions are as follows:

Openers

The captain sends out his first two batsmen — known as the openers — and one of these must face the first ball. Openers tend to be solid and fairly steady scorers, like Australia's Justin Langer and the great West Indies pairing of Desmond Haynes and Gordon Greenidge, or South Africa's Graeme Smith.

Number three

The number three batsman is the keystone of the batting order, and usually the most technically adept cricketer in the side. If he fails, the team may fail. Great number threes in history include Brian Lara of the West Indies, Sachin Tendulkar of India and Ricky Ponting of Australia.

Numbers four and five

The other specialist batsmen have the responsibility to build solid innings once the foundations of the side have been laid by the first three batsmen. Some people argue that these roles are easier to fill as the openers have taken the sting out of the main bowlers — who usually bowl in 'spells' of seven or eight overs at a time before having a rest while the captain brings on alternative bowlers.

Number six/wicketkeeper

The sixth batting position is sometimes filled by a wicketkeeper, but this role also calls for batting expertise – like the skills of Adam Gilchrist of Australia, Alan Knott of England and Mark Boucher of South Africa.

Number seven/all rounder

The number seven in cricket is the champagne star of the side – Ian Botham, Imran Khan, Kapil Dev and Andrew Flintoff all played at number seven at various stages of their careers and all excelled with bat and ball, often turning an innings around when the 'recognised' batsmen had failed.

Numbers eight to eleven

Collectively known as 'the tail end', these batsmen can often make the valuable runs that turn a good total into a great one. But equally, they can collapse like a house of cards. It's never a good idea to rely on the tail to get a team out of trouble.

Pocket Fact

Never underestimate a number eight. Australian Jason Gillespie, playing for his country against Bangladesh in 2006, was moved up the batting order from his usual position of number eight (or lower) to act as 'night watchman' – a lower-order batsman who is sent in to bat in preference to recognised batsmen late in a day's play. He went on to score 201 not out, the highest score ever made by a night watchman in test cricket.

3

THE CRICKET KIT BAG

*It's typical of cricket that the only people who get to wear black trousers
— the umpires — are the ones who aren't going to get their clothes dirty.*
Anonymous

At its simplest, cricket is a game that requires nothing more than
a set of stumps chalked on a wall, a piece of wood for a bat and
any old ball. But equally it can involve huge wheeled bags
crammed full of safety gear and other accessories. In this chapter
we look at the game's essential kit — and at some of the key skills
you'll need once you've bought it.

THE BAT

Basics

Bats are made up of two parts, the handle and the blade. The
blade, which is the main part of the bat, is wooden — and almost
always taken from the willow tree, because of its tough, shock-
absorbent quality. The handle, made from wood or cane, is fixed
into a recess in the blade and then glued in place. The handle is
bound with twine and then covered with a rubber grip to make it
easier to grasp.

Pocket Fact

*If you're choosing a bat for a junior and want to get the size
right, follow the rule that bats should come to the top of the thigh
when stood against the leg. Don't be tempted to buy a bigger bat
for a junior to 'grow into' as this will harm technique.*

History

Bats evolved from a traditional club or cudgel shape in the earliest days of the game when all bowling was underarm and the weight and thickness of the bat needed to be concentrated at the bottom. By the mid-19th century, when round-arm and overarm bowling became the norm, bats were of a style and shape very similar to those used today. As we saw in Chapter 2, the maximum height and width of the bat is strictly governed by the laws of cricket.

Choice

Devotees of Harry Potter will remember the lengths wizards go to in selecting the right wand to match the user – bats are pretty much the same, with the levels of wizardry on a par if the right bat is in the right hands. Whether you opt for Sachin Tendulkar's hefty club or the feather-light delicacy of David Gower's lighter bat, the key is to get something that suits your physique and abilities. But as a general rule, start light and work up to the heavier bats. If you're relying on the bat to do the work, it means something's missing from your technique.

Knocking in

Although the days of lovingly oiling a bat are largely behind us thanks to protective coatings and superior craftsmanship, it is still necessary to prepare a bat for first use. A bat without a protective cover should be treated with a little linseed oil occasionally, but not over-oiled as this can cause the bat to rot. All bats, however, should be 'knocked-in'. You can do this with an old cricket ball. An hour or so of gently knocking the soft older ball against the bat will help to firm up the 'face' of the bat and will make it even more effective when you come to use it in action. When storing a bat, make sure you don't leave it in damp conditions, and be especially careful to keep the bottom end dry, as water penetration can soak upwards from the base of the bat and split it.

● THE BALL ●

Basics

The standard red cricket ball has a cork heart encased in tightly wound string and then covered by two (or sometimes four) pieces of leather stitched together along a wide seam. This seam is essential for medium-paced bowlers who grip the ball with their index and fore-finger either side of the seam and use this to vary the direction of the ball – swinging it in towards the batsman or away. It's also critical for spin bowlers, who use the seam to help their wrist or hand action in turning the ball one way or the other off the pitch. In addition, the ball of two halves allows the fielding side to 'smooth' one half by shining it repeatedly while ignoring the rough surface of the other half. This has the effect of making the ball swing in the air as the smooth half has less wind resistance when the ball is bowled.

History

Cricket balls have been made in a form approximating their current make-up since at least 1760. The laws of 1744 laid down the maximum size and dimensions (see p. 18 for more detail) and thereafter the limits for the ball were pretty fixed. Few of the changes to the game down the years have impacted on the ball itself but one-day cricket – especially the day/night variation of the game played under floodlights – is now played with a white ball to improve visibility against the colourful array of back-grounds and clothing worn in the limited overs game. The MCC has been experimenting with a pink ball which is expected to be an improvement on the current white variant.

Pocket Fact ✎

No innovation in ball technology has been quite as simple or as popular as the invention of the tapeball. Extremely popular in Pakistan and India – the ball in question is often a tennis ball brought up to the desired weight by being wrapped in brightly coloured sticky tape. It's a relatively recent innovation – made popular in the last 20 years or so.

Choice

Like bats, cricket balls come in junior sizes, but it can be great practice for a young player to become familiar with the size and weight of a full-size match ball as this can have a major impact on bowling style and fielding technique. For the very young player, plastic alternatives – such as those used in Kwik-Cricket, a form of the game devised exclusively for very young players – allow young cricketers to become familiar with the basics of the game without too much risk of injury.

● THE PADS ●

Basics

Cricket pads can look pretty ungainly, but anyone who's been struck on the knee by a cricket ball would swear by their use. There are two types of pads – those for batting, with protection for the entire lower leg, knee and lower part of the thigh, and those for keeping wicket, which have lower leg and knee protection only, but are much easier to wear while squatting.

History

Pads didn't feature much in early cricket matches – although an underarm delivery can still cause a fair amount of injury, especially when bowled on an uneven surface. Round-arm deliveries made the pad an essential accessory and the first were very rudimentary jobs, fashioned from wood. Pads as we know them today were introduced in the mid-19th century.

Choice

Until about 30 years ago all pads were buckle-fastened and the small metal catches were prone to slip open at the worst possible moment – such as when a batsman was halfway down the pitch chasing a quick run – but fortunately all modern pads now use Velcro fastenings which make them much more effective. Modern pads are also considerably lighter and more flexible.

Pocket Fact

Indian cricket legend Sachin Tendulkar was given a pair of pads by his hero Sunil Gavaskar when he was just a schoolboy.

● THE GLOVES ●

Basics

Gloves also come in two types – larger gloves with extra padding and webbing for the wicketkeeper and smaller batting gloves with sausage-like padding on each finger and extra protection for the thumb of whichever hand the batsman places at the bottom of his grip of the bat (batting gloves are available for both left and right handed batsmen). Good gloves are essential as hands are particularly vulnerable when batting.

History

Like pads, gloves were introduced when cricket ceased to be a game played predominantly along the ground. The development of hard, bouncy pitches and overarm bowling spelled a boom in protective clothing.

Pocket Fact

It is against the laws of cricket for fielders (except the wicketkeeper) to wear gloves of any kind – even in an English county match in March!

● THE 'WHITES' ●

Basics

The clothing that is worn in cricket depends on the format of the game that's being played. First-class cricket normally dictates that all players should wear white trousers, a white shirt and a white long or short sleeved sweater – with coloured piping around the v-neck. The limited overs game is now often played in brightly coloured 'pyjama' kits – a fashion which owes more to selling replica shirts than to any serious attempt to break from the tradition of 'whites'.

History

White clothing might seem like a strange choice in a game where you are guaranteed to spend a lot of time scrabbling around on the grass trying to stop a ball. But the logic of cricket whites depends on your perspective – it makes perfect sense to wear white clothing if this allows the red ball to be seen clearly by all participants and it's also very logical to wear white in the open air in mid summer to mitigate the worst of the sun's rays. But when you're washing a whole team's kit every week, it's probably a different story. What we do know is that white (or at least a clotted cream-like off-white) is and has always been the uniform of first-class cricket.

Pocket Fact

To remove grass stains from whites try using a stain remover, or mix together a paste of washing powder and water to gently scrub the stain with before washing on a hot setting. If the stain persists, rub on some dilute methylated spirit. Never iron over a stain as it will make it much harder to shift.

Choice

Modern fabric technology has revolutionised the weight and performance of clothing, but the traditional 'look' of the modern cricketer is pretty similar to his 19th century predecessor. Nowadays, the chunky woollen sweater is likely to have been replaced by a lightweight polyester version and the flannels of yesteryear are now closer to jogging bottoms in style and substance.

🏏 THE BAG 🏏

Basics

There are two types of bags in popular use – a backpack style bag which is light enough to carry on the shoulder and big enough to carry a bat, a set of pads, gloves, whites and shoes, and a larger bag that is colloquially known by the name of the object it most resembles – a coffin – which professionals use as a rule because they are so much bigger and can hold all the necessary equipment for a day's play, plus spares. Coffins are often wheeled to make it easier to drag them around cricket grounds.

🏏 PROTECTION AND SAFETY 🏏

Cricket is a fast and furious game, and even the gentlest ball can cause severe damage if it catches the edge of the bat and clouts the batsman in the face, so protective equipment has become essential kit these days. Here are some of the must-haves for your kit bag.

- **Helmet.** Many people use these now – although they are still optional – as they are especially critical when facing fast bowling. The England and Wales Cricket Board states that all young players under the age of 18 should wear a helmet as a matter of course when batting. It should be appropriately sized and a decent tight fit. Before you put your helmet on, make sure the faceguard is properly adjusted to give you maximum protection against a flying ball – you should not be able to pass a ball between the space from faceguard to the peak of the helmet. Remember also that helmets should be worn when fielding close to the bat (particularly at short leg).

Pocket Fact 🏏

One of the finest achievements as a bowler is to claim a hat trick – three wickets in successive balls. The term is said to have originated in the 1850s when H Stephenson achieved the feat playing for All England and was rewarded with a commemorative hat. The term has spread to mark an individual's three goals in football and hockey.

- **Thigh pad.** Gone are the days when a paperback book in the pocket would suffice. Nowadays a thigh pad, strapped to the inner thigh with Velcro, offers protection to the upper leg beyond that afforded by the pads. It is especially useful when facing fast bowling.

- **Shoes.** Traditional cricket spikes are becoming increasingly rare, but shoes with a good grip are very important – especially to a bowler. Even if you don't go for traditional metal spikes, choose shoes with rubber dimples that have some tread – normal trainers will have you sliding around all over the place.

- **Box.** All male cricketers should wear a box – a moulded plastic cup that covers the genitals and groin – preferably within a jockstrap to stop it moving around when running. Box etiquette dictates that you should never borrow someone else's – and you may not fancy rooting around in a communal kitbag for one either. This is something to buy yourself.

- **Armguard.** When the ball rises sharply from the pitch – for example if a fast bowler is bowling a lot of short balls, or if there's a lot of uneven bounce from the pitch, it's a good idea to use an armguard to protect the forearm from bruising (or worse).

- **Shin pads.** Not just part of the footballer's kit bag, these are vital if you're a close fielder in positions such as silly point and short leg.

Internet shopping

Cricket equipment isn't always easy to source in the larger sports outlets, so the growth of the internet has made life a lot easier for the cricket enthusiast who wants to get hold of a good deal. Among the many decent equipment websites are the following:

www.cricketdirect.co.uk
www.cricketsupplies.com
www.amazon.co.uk (and variations worldwide)
www.owzat-cricket.co.uk

● STAYING SAFE AND FIT ●

The equipment you use makes a big difference, but there are other ways to prepare for a hard day's cricket that will help you stay safe and secure on the field of play:

- **Warm up well.** It may not look like the hardest impact sport in the world, but cricket strains muscles and joints, especially if you're bowling or keeping wicket. So a good warm-up routine is a must. Ten to 15 minutes of jogging and stretching exercises will loosen you up sufficiently for a day in the field. If you are a bowler, focus on warming up side and shoulder muscles before you start turning your arm over.

- **Slip, slop, slap.** Not a children's TV programme, but an advertising campaign first popularised in Australia as a way of raising awareness of skin cancer. The slogan emphasises the need to slip on a shirt, slop on the sun cream and slap on a hat. Most cricketers won't need too much encouragement to do the first of these, but sun block or high factor cream and a suitable sun hat are safety essentials for any lengthy exposure to the sun, whether the day is scorching hot or not. White zinc sun block – the stuff that resembles lipstick – is popular among cricketers from Australia and other very hot countries.

- **Drink plenty.** This is less about the pub after the game and more about the long session of fielding when players can rapidly dehydrate. Assuming you're spending around two to three hours per session in the field, you should factor in at least one break for water or squash for all the fielders and batsmen.

- **Warm down well (as well).** Going straight off to celebrate after a famous victory is a sure way to wake up the next day with a chronic muscle ache. A gentle warm down will help you stretch out all the tension that's built up in your muscles over the day. Again, five to 10 minutes of stretches and a gentle jog should do it – and it's a lot less painful than the alternative.

Mettle and metal

Dennis Lillee may have been a legend in Australia for his fast bowling prowess and his 355 test match wickets, but he will also be long remembered for an extraordinary incident connected to an aluminium bat he used in the first test match against England in December 1979. He came out to bat at the WACA ground in Western Australia carrying a bat made from aluminium – created by an associate of his. After he had hit a ball for three runs, the umpires were approached by England captain Mike Brearley who requested Lillee change the bat for fear of damaging the ball. At the same time, Lillee's own captain Greg Chappell sent out a replacement bat for Lillee as Chappell thought the ball should have gone for four and that his bat was faulty. Lillee responded to this two-pronged assault on his innovation by throwing his bat towards the pavilion in fury and there was a 10-minute hiatus while he calmed down.

Sales of aluminium bats thrived after the incident, but alas the laws were soon amended to ensure all bats should be made of wood. This theory was tested to the limit by another Australian legend, Ricky Ponting, who played with a bat reinforced with a carbon graphite strip on the back. Although Ponting used the bat for some time, its design was eventually outlawed by the ICC in 2006.

● THE KEY SKILLS ●

Having the right equipment is only part of the story for the would-be cricketer. Learning the skills of the game takes a long time and it can be years before you feel you are comfortable with bat or ball. Here's a brief overview of some of the essentials when playing the game.

BATTING

- **Your grip.** Hold the bat handle so that the inverted 'v-shape' between the thumb and forefinger of your top hand (the left hand for a right-handed batsman) is in a line with the outside edge of the bat. This will help you keep your forearm straight when hitting the ball.

- **Your head.** Keep your head still and watch the ball all the way from the bowler's hand to the bat.

- **Your feet.** Keep your feet a comfortable distance apart and your knees slightly bent to allow you to move forward or back quickly.

- **Your bat.** Many batsmen these days prefer to hold their bats at right angles to the body while awaiting the ball. This 'back-lift' is regarded as being good for shot selection and power.

- **Your choice of shot.** This is determined by such a wide range of factors that it's almost impossible to advise, but in general try to judge the pace and bounce of the pitch and the bowler's action by defending a few shots in the early part of your innings. This is known as 'getting your eye in' – adjusting to the conditions before playing attacking shots. Attacking shots in front of the wicket are drives, behind the wicket they are cuts (on the off side), pulls or hooks (on the leg side).

BOWLING

- **Fast bowling.** Great fast bowlers have an almost mechanical rhythm – their pace and accuracy is honed by many hours of practice in the cricket nets. Genuine pace is a mixture of the speed generated by the run-up to the wicket, the speed of the action as the bowler turns his arm over his head and the release and 'follow through' – the final part of the run after the ball has been delivered. If you can get this action into a flowing movement and manage to get the ball to hit the ground in the right spot, you've got the makings of a great 'quickie'.

- **Spin bowling.** This has less to do with the rhythm of the run-up and more with how you grip the ball and what you do as you release it. The best spin bowlers can deceive the batsman into thinking the ball will spin one way when it hits the ground when in fact it spins the other – there are many popular names for this kind of delivery, including the 'googly'.

- **Swing/seam bowling.** The third type of bowling doesn't just rely on out-and-out pace for its variation, it also uses the seam and surface of the ball to swing the ball in the air or move it off the pitch.

- **Line and length.** Bowling is about forcing the batsman to make a mistake. If your deliveries hit the pitch in line with the batsman's off stump and on a length that makes it difficult for him to decide whether to play forward or back, you are making life very hard and will eventually force his hand. Practise bowling in the nets, using a plastic marker on a good length and see how often you can hit it.

Pocket Fact

An under-rated skill of cricket is the ability to run well between the wickets. Many leading players have been undone in this way – notably England's Owais Shah and Australia's Shane Watson. The key is to take the first run at speed which gives more time to assess further runs. Calling is also essential – calls like 'yes', 'no' or 'one run' are clear signals, while 'go' sounds too much like 'no' and should be avoided.

FIELDING

- **Fitness.** You might think that cricket is a sedate game in which you can get away with a wobbly belly and very little running. You'd be wrong. Racing a ball to the boundary involves strength and good sprinting skills. Equally, a long afternoon of fielding requires stamina and, most of all, lots of concentration.

- **A keen eye.** Whether you're catching the ball or just stopping a hard shot you need to keep your focus. If you are distracted from the ball's progress at any point you risk dropping it, or being hit by it.

- **Soft hands.** Catching a cricket ball may seem daunting, but if you think of your hands as a soft pouch for the ball, like interlocking cups which relax slightly just on the point of contact with the ball, you should avoid the slap of stinging leather. Remember the maxim – catches win matches.

- **A good throwing arm.** A strong arm is essential if you're fielding on or near the boundary.

- **Be positive.** While the bowler is running in to deliver the ball, take a couple of steps towards the action. Known as 'walking-in' – this keeps you moving and ready to respond should the ball be heading your way.

Pocket Fact

Designer bats (see above) aren't the only innovation ever trialled in cricket. In 1963, a group of cricketers staged an exhibition match at Lord's in London to experiment with a fourth stump as part of a proposal to make the game more attractive. The theory was that a fourth stump would give the bowler more to aim at and therefore would encourage more attacking play from the batsman, who couldn't simply block every ball. This idea has been suggested many times, even at the highest level – such as by New Zealand legend Martin Crowe. But as yet, it has never been successfully shown to be of benefit to the game.

4

THE FIELD OF PLAY

There is scarcely a part of the globe that has not witnessed cricket in one form or another: every continent – including Antarctica, up mountain, down valley, on sea and on land, on beach and on pavement, outdoors and indoors.
David Rayvern Allen

The great Australian Don Bradman once noted that cricket is an easy game when it's played on the ground. That might be true if you're a batsman, but it's only made possible by the extraordinary efforts of the people who produce the pitches, squares and out-fields that make up the entire field of play. In this chapter we focus on the grass roots of cricket – quite literally – as we look at the pitch, the world's greatest grounds and the impact of the weather on playing conditions.

Pocket Fact

Not all cricket grounds have the oval shape taken by two of the earliest sites – Lord's and the Oval in London, England. Some grounds are completely circular with an even boundary distance all round. The Oval is, obviously, most famous for its shape – which was only created by a road that was built around the ground in the 1790s.

● THE CRICKET FIELD ●

The playing area is notionally divided into sections – known as infield and outfield – which are useful for field placement, but which also have a significance in limited overs cricket, where rules govern how many fielders can be in specific positions.

THE CRICKET FIELD

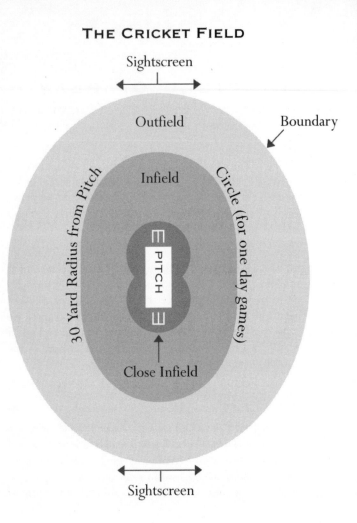

Cricket field terminology

Here's a brief overview of the main terminology of the cricket field:

- **Pitch/wicket.** *The word 'pitch' is used to refer to the carefully prepared strip with wickets at either end at the very centre of the field of play. This area is also commonly known as the wicket.*
- **Square.** *This is a larger rectangular prepared area in the centre of the ground.*
- **Infield.** *This is an area of the ground within a 30-yard radius of the wickets. It is marked in limited overs cricket as there are restrictions on the number of fielders that can be used outside this 'zone' (see Chapter 6 for more information).*
- **Outfield**. *This term describes the area from the edge of the infield to the boundary.*
- **Groundsman.** *The individual who is responsible for the preparation, maintenance and general upkeep of the pitch and the whole ground.*

PREPARATION AND NATURE

The area of the ground which requires the greatest level of preparation is the wicket. Before a game is played it will be regularly mowed, watered, rolled and kept protected from the weather. Although it is technically a grassed area, it is often clay brown and spongy in texture, more like compacted mud than the lush green outfield. In general terms there are three main types of wicket preparation:

- **'Green' wickets.** Wickets that are under-prepared are sometimes known as 'green'. This is often regarded as an aid to fast bowlers as it makes bounce from the wicket quite unpredictable.

- **'True' wickets.** A wicket that has an even covering of grass that has been prepared under normal conditions will play in a predictable manner. This is good news for the batsmen who will be able to choose their shots with a greater degree of certainty.

- **'Dry' or 'cracked' wickets.** These are wickets that are already beginning to lose the flatness of the surface before the game has begun. This type of wicket will be very good news for spin bowlers who can use the cracks in the wicket to make the ball deviate.

Many wickets will change their nature over the course of a test match – from an even or true surface to a very badly cracked surface that will be suited to spin bowling on the last couple of days of the match. This is something a captain has to take into account when deciding whether to bat or bowl first at the beginning of the game.

Pocket Fact

In December 1878, two teams from Cambridge University played one of the few recorded games of cricket on ice – not in the middle of a lake, but on a frozen field at the water meadows of Grantchester near the town.

Regional patterns

Different parts of the world are well known for the varying nature of their pitches – mainly due to differences in climate and the demands of the local teams:

- In India, Bangladesh and Pakistan the wickets often take spin throughout the game.

- In Australia and West Indies, many wickets are hard and flat and so favour fast bowling.

- In England, South Africa and Sri Lanka many wickets are traditionally regarded as good batting tracks, producing lots of runs but also more drawn games.

Pocket Fact ✎

It is against the laws of cricket for players to practise on the pitch itself before a game. Players may use the outfield and even the square, but they must stop practising 30 minutes before the start of play.

⚫ GREAT GROUNDS OF THE WORLD ⚫

Everyone who plays or watches cricket has their own favourite ground, often for very subjective reasons – a memory of a great innings, of a great view or just a great atmosphere. Here's a selection of the finest grounds around the world.

AUSTRALIA

- **Melbourne Cricket Ground (MCG).** The largest cricket ground in the world with a capacity of 100,000. Cricket was first played at Melbourne in 1854 and the ground has played host to some famous landmark events in cricket – the first test match in 1877 and the centenary match in 1977, the first one-day international in 1971 and, outside of cricket, it was one of the venues for the 1956 Olympic Games.

- **Sydney Cricket Ground (SCG).** Cricket was first played at the SCG in 1878. For many years it had a reputation as a great batting track, with some of the finest innings in history made here, including an incredible 452 not out by Don Bradman – his highest first-class score. Now, though, it is regarded as a better bowler's wicket, with spinners finding particular success.

- **Adelaide.** Although it is the junior partner of the 'big two' grounds of Sydney and Melbourne, Adelaide is by far the most beautiful ground in Australia, noted for its picturesque setting and fine architecture. The Adelaide Oval has been in use as a cricket ground since the 1860s and is regarded as a fine batting track.

Six of the best – grounds which have hosted the most test matches:

1. *Lord's, London, England (121 test matches)**
2. *Melbourne, Australia (102 test matches)**
3. *Sydney, Australia (98 test matches)**
4. *The Oval, London, England (93 test matches)**
5. *Old Trafford, Manchester, England (74 test matches)**
6. *Headingley, Leeds, England (70 test matches)**

*to November 2010

BANGLADESH

- **Mirpur.** The Shere Bangla National Stadium was founded in 2006 and saw its first test cricket in the game versus India in 2007. The stadium was originally designed for football and so it has been extensively remodelled to take on an oval shape as a dedicated cricketing arena. Extensive drainage was installed during the remodelling which makes it a ground that's relatively unaffected by weather conditions.

- **Chittagong.** Another of Bangladesh's bespoke test match stadia, Chittagong first saw test match cricket in 2006 in the game against Sri Lanka.

ENGLAND

- **Lord's.** Famous for being the home of the MCC, Lord's is regarded as the unofficial home of cricket. It was founded in 1814 by Thomas Lord. Although it's not the oldest or largest ground in the world, it occupies a unique place in the heart of cricketers worldwide. Batsmen who score a century and bowlers who take five or more wickets in an innings have their names added to the ground's honours board.

Pocket Fact

Lord's is also home to the world's oldest cricket museum.

- **Trent Bridge.** Founded by one of cricket's early entrepreneurs, William Clarke, in the late 1830s, Trent Bridge became a vital meeting point for cricketers from the north and south of England. As one of the smallest test cricket venues it retains an intimacy and a link with its heritage.

- **Headingley.** The home of Yorkshire cricket, it is a curious place with little discernible architectural merit, but a long and distinguished history of fantastic cricketing endeavour. Established in 1890, it first saw test cricket in 1899 and has seen some of the finest games since – including two Bradman treble-hundreds and Geoff Boycott's hundredth hundred (in 1977) as well as remarkable games in the 1981 and 2001 Ashes test series.

Pocket Fact

The Oval cricket ground in London was the site of the first test match between England and Australia on English soil, in 1880. It was also the site of the catastrophic England collapse two years later which led to the creation of 'The Ashes' – see p.116.

INDIA

- **Mumbai.** The Wankhede Stadium in Mumbai is the third ground in the city to host international cricket matches. It took over the mantle of test arena from the Brabourne Stadium in 1974 and has seen some impressive performances since then, including England's Ian Botham showing his all-round expertise (a century and 13 wickets) in the 1980 Jubilee test and Indian legend Ravi Shastri scoring six sixes in an over in 1984 – then, only the second batsman in history to achieve this feat.

- **Chennai.** The MA Chidambaram Stadium (known locally as Chepauk) is famous for its incredible atmosphere and intelligent, appreciative crowds. It was founded in 1916 and first hosted a test match in 1934 against England. The first ever game in the Indian domestic competition the Ranji Trophy was also played here.

- **Bangalore.** The M Chinnaswamy Stadium in Bangalore had an inauspicious start to its test match career as the first game it hosted in 1974 was played against a backdrop of half-finished stands. However, it has recovered to play host to some terrific milestones, most notably Indian spinner Anil Kumble's 400th test match wicket.

NEW ZEALAND

- **Wellington.** Cricket was first played at the Basin Reserve in Wellington in 1868, and it became a test match arena in 1930. It is a stunning ground in the heart of the city which has seen some notable landmarks, including New Zealanders Martin Crowe and Andrew Jones scoring a massive 467-run third wicket stand against Sri Lanka in 1990. It was also the site of the country's legendary all-rounder Richard Hadlee's 300th test wicket.

- **Christchurch.** The AMI Stadium is New Zealand's most historic cricket ground, with a playing history dating back to 1882. The first test match was staged in 1930 and since then it has been a regular test match ground. The stadium has a very large capacity, but manages to retain an intimacy that marks it out as a very popular venue for spectators.

- **Auckland.** Eden Park in Auckland has played host to test cricket since 1930 and the ground is famous for a significant high and low point in New Zealand's cricketing history. On the plus side, it was the venue for the country's first test victory – against the West Indies in the 1955–1956 season – but it was also the scene of the test side's most humiliating total, a mere 26 all out against England in 1955.

Pocket Fact ━━━━

Many cricket grounds around the world have their equivalent long rooms, but Lord's has the original — a long seating area that players walk through on their way from the dressing room to the field, exchanging comments with members along the way. England cricketer David Steele once famously got lost on his way out to bat after passing through the Long Room.

PAKISTAN

- **Lahore.** The Gaddafi Stadium first saw test match cricket in 1959 when Pakistan went up against Australia. With a modern design and a massive capacity of 60,000, it is an impressive arena that has played host to some impressive displays, most notably the 1996 World Cup final. It was also the first stadium in Pakistan to have floodlights.

- **Karachi.** The National Stadium is the spiritual home of Pakistan cricket and one of the liveliest arenas in the Asian area. It began life as a test match ground in 1955 against India and has been the scene of many great tussles, though in recent years security concerns have limited visitors from outside of the Asian countries. Karachi was known as a 'fortress' as Pakistan were unbeaten on the ground from 1955–2000.

- **Faisalabad.** The Iqbal Stadium is notable for many reasons. It hosted its first test match in 1978 against India, but it is legendary for its potentially devastating weather conditions, with fog and bad light a constant peril. The ground was also the venue for a different kind of storm, when England's Mike Gatting clashed with umpire Shakoor Rana in 1987 (see p.144).

SOUTH AFRICA

- **Cape Town.** Newlands stands at the foot of Table Mountain and is rightly regarded as one of the most exquisite places in the world to play cricket. The first test match played here was in 1889 v England and since then it has been a firm favourite among players and spectators. It's a unique ground in other ways in that it's the only ground in South Africa that is specifically designed to suit spin bowling.

- **Johannesburg.** The Wanderers Stadium can legitimately lay claim to the status of legend as it has seen some of the most outstanding moments of cricket since it was first used for test matches in 1956. From South African legend Graeme Pollock's 274 against Australia in 1966–1967 to England captain Mike Atherton batting for 10 hours to save a match in 1995, Johannesburg has seen it all – but perhaps nothing caps the remarkable one-day match in March 2006 when South Africa successfully overcame Australia's record-breaking total of 434.

- **Centurion.** A relative newcomer to the test arena – the first international game was played here in 1995 against England – but SuperSport Park has become a real favourite due to its combination of excellent facilities for the players and staff and an incredibly relaxed family atmosphere helped enormously by the huge grass mounds that form part of the seating area. It also has a reputation as a good batsman's wicket.

SRI LANKA

- **Colombo.** The R Premadasa Stadium was built in 1986 and first hosted a test match in 1992 against Australia. It is the largest stadium in Sri Lanka, with a capacity of 35,000. This venue was the scene of the highest test match innings of 952–6 declared by Sri Lanka against India in 1997–1998, with Sri Lanka legend Sanath Jayasuriya top-scoring with 340.

- **Galle.** The Galle International Stadium has a story to tell that is totally unconnected with cricket, but which makes it a remarkable venue all the same. First used for test cricket in 1998 v New Zealand, it was an incredibly beautiful and elegant ground, when it was destroyed by the tsunami of 2004. It was lovingly rebuilt with the support of many international cricket stars, including spinners Shane Warne and Muttiah Muralitharan, who both cited Galle as one of their favourite grounds.

Pocket Fact

If you're watching stadium cricket, the best seats are often behind the bowler at either end of the ground – to the sides of the sightscreen. From here you can gauge the movement of the ball and catch most of the action. You can still enjoy the game watching 'side on', but it's harder to pick up the flight of the ball.

WEST INDIES

- **Barbados.** The Kensington Oval is a ground steeped in West Indies cricket history. It hosted the first test match in the West Indies in 1930, but before that it was the host of many touring sides, dating back as far as 1895. In recent times it has been used as the venue for the 2007 World Cup final.

- **Jamaica.** Sabina Park is a ground that has a chequered history, but which has played a vital part in the development of West Indies cricket. Test matches were first played in 1930 against England and the ground witnessed West Indies legend Gary Sobers make the 365 which stood for many years as the highest total in test cricket from 1958 to 1994, when it was beaten by another West Indian, Brian Lara. It was also the venue of a test match against England in January 1998 which had to be abandoned after just 62 balls had been bowled because of safety concerns (see weather stopped play, below). Sabina Park is a hard, flat track which suited the hostility of the great fast bowlers of the 1970s and 1980s.

- **Trinidad.** The Queen's Park Oval is one of the most beautiful in the West Indies, and also one of the largest. It first staged test cricket in 1930 and was the famous location of the destruction of the England team for a dismal 46 all out in 1994–1995. Fans at the stadium have a reputation for creating an unbeatable party atmosphere.

ZIMBABWE

- **Harare.** The Harare Sports Club is the main arena in Zimbabwe, which first hosted a test match in 1992 against India.

It is another city-centre ground, within picturesque surroundings in the nation's capital city.

- **Bulawayo.** The Queens Sports Club is another beautiful arena, which is surrounded by grass embankments for its spectators. It was first used as a test match arena in 1994 v Sri Lanka.

Pocket Fact

The title of world's oldest permanent cricket ground is one that is hotly disputed, with at least three clubs in the south of England laying claim to the honour. They are Mitcham CC in Surrey (which claims to have been hosting cricket since 1685), Firle in Sussex (1725) and The Vine Cricket Ground in Kent (1734).

WEATHER STOPS PLAY

Rain and bad light are pretty standard conditions that can cause a day's cricket to be delayed, curtailed or even abandoned altogether. Following recent changes to the laws, the decision to stop play rests solely with the umpires. As outlined in the Laws of Cricket it is left to the umpires alone to determine whether the playing surface has become dangerous – especially if a bowler cannot get a secure foothold and the batsmen or fielders cannot run safely. In practice light showers shouldn't cause a break in play and many umpires have allowed play to continue in failing light, especially if the game is close to conclusion. But the game is littered with exceptional circumstances which have led to breaks of a very different nature – some natural and some wholly unnatural. Here are some of the most famous examples:

- **Fog stops play.** Faisalabad, December 1998. The Pakistan v Zimbabwe test match was abandoned without a ball being bowled owing to an unseasonable covering of thick fog which blanketed the ground until the final afternoon.

- **Snow stops play.** Buxton Derbyshire, June 1975. The Derbyshire v Lancashire County Championship match was already remarkable for the fact that more than 500 runs had been scored on the first day of a three-day domestic league match (477 of them by Lancashire), but when day two of the game dawned, the ground was covered in an inch of snow. Heavy snow continued throughout the morning and the day's play was abandoned at lunchtime. Amazingly, the game produced a result as Derbyshire were bowled out twice on the third and final day for scores of 42 and 87 respectively.

- **Pitch stops play.** Kingston Jamaica, January 1998. England opened their innings against the West Indies and were soon in trouble. By the end of the first hour's play they'd lost three wickets and scored 17 runs. The physiotherapist had been called to the pitch six times to treat injuries caused by the uneven and erratic bounce from the newly laid pitch. The umpires decided to abandon the match before anyone got seriously injured.

- **Bees stop play.** Kandy, December 2007. In the first test match between Sri Lanka and England, a swarm of bees hovered over the wicket, causing batsmen, fielders and officials to flatten themselves against the ground and take evasive action until the threat had passed.

Pocket Fact

The Skate Bank cricket match is played on a sand bank in the Moray Firth, Scotland, which only appears when there's a combination of very low tides and high pressure weather systems. The last attempt to play the game was in August 2010, which was only partially successful as the water remained ankle deep.

5

THE ETIQUETTE OF CRICKET

To go into a cricket match for nothing but cricket is as though a man were to go into an inn for nothing but drink.
Neville Cardus

In this chapter we look at the very broad idea of cricket's etiquette, including some of the finer traditions of the game and some examples of what happens when the competition on the field becomes a little too fraught.

● DO THE RIGHT THING ●

There are certain standards expected of anyone who plays cricket. The laws and spirit of the game define the right way to play, but there's something more ethereal about the etiquette of the game. Cricket etiquette is bound up with the traditional notion of gentility or good manners that is often seen as old-fashioned or fussy. But for the true cricketer etiquette is more about enjoying the whole experience of the game rather than simply trying to produce a result. Cricket is, after all, how most players choose to spend their one day of rest per week – so it might as well be fun, too.

● ETIQUETTE ON THE FIELD ● OF PLAY

The following is not an exhaustive list, as the specifics of etiquette tend to differ between nations and levels of the game, but they are a good benchmark for how things should be done. Some might seem silly and some quite antiquated, but they all contribute to a positive atmosphere.

- **The toss.** At the toss the captain of the home team should produce a coin, toss it and allow the opposition captain to call 'heads or tails'.

- **Start of the game.** At the beginning of the first innings, the umpires should be first out onto the field of play, followed by the fielding team and then finally by the opening batsmen.

- **The bowler's mark.** When the bowler marks his run-up to the wicket, he should strive to avoid damaging the ground by dragging studs or spikes across the turf. It shows a general lack of respect to the ground staff and is unnecessary if he has use of a small, spiked marker which is readily available.

- **Incoming batsmen.** If a wicket falls, the incoming batsman should be applauded by the fielding side when he reaches the square. This applause is often prompted by the captain or a senior player calling 'man in'.

- **Run outs.** When a batsman isn't facing the ball he is often preparing for a run by standing on the edge of (or just outside of) his crease. If he and his bat are fully outside he can be run out by the bowler. In practice, the bowler should warn the batsman by holding the ball over the stumps, but not by actually running him out.

Pocket Fact

Australian opening batsman Bill Brown was run out in this fashion by India all-rounder Vinoo Mankad in the second test match at Sydney in 1947–1948. Since that controversial incident, the act of running out the non-striking batsman in this way is known as a 'Mankad'.

- **Appeals.** It is considered extremely bad practice to appeal for a dismissal when you as a bowler or as a fielder know that the batsman was not out. This is an attempt to sway the umpire with the power of your voice and will most likely be met with even more stubborn resistance next time a genuine appeal is made.

- **Walking.** Equally, it is good practice for a batsman, when he knows he has hit the ball and is out caught behind the wicket to walk from the field of play before the umpire is forced to make a decision. This is rare in international cricket, which is a great loss to that form of the game.

Pocket Fact

Walking is a contentious issue, with the cricketing world split along two lines — those who feel it is the batsman's responsibility to admit he is out and those who feel it is the umpire's duty to make the decision. Some argue that too much is at stake in the professional game for individuals to willingly give away their wicket.

- **Respect for the umpires.** The laws state that the umpire's decision is final. Any abuse, criticism or maltreatment of the umpire is inexcusable. It is the captain's responsibility to ensure this is honoured by all players.

- **Respect for the pitch.** Members of the fielding side must never run across the pitch between overs or otherwise do anything with the intention of damaging the pitch, square or any part of the playing surface.

- **Damaging the ball.** No player may damage or deface the ball in any way — for example by rubbing it with grit or attempting to lift the seam with a surreptitious fingernail.

- **Time wasting.** If anyone wastes time on the fielding side, the umpire will warn them twice and then will take action by awarding five penalty runs to the batting side.

- **Sledging** (intimidating the batsman). This is a common practice, ranging in ferocity from a bit of friendly banter to a full-on attack by fielders intent on breaking the batsman's concentration. The only possible result of this is that they do the same to you when you're batting and the game descends into a slanging match.

Pocket Fact

There are many occasional jibes between professionals that get picked up by the TV stations' stump microphones. A classic 'sledge' came from Australian wicketkeeper Rod Marsh to England's Ian Botham. The latter had just come to the wicket and was focusing on his innings when Marsh said: 'So how's your wife and my kids?'

- **The scoreboard.** The home team should be responsible for maintaining the scoreboard throughout the game. Both teams should provide a representative to keep the scorebooks up to date.

- **Spectators.** The spectators should never go on to the ground, nor should they shout at any officials or players. They can clap, though.

Supporters' clubs

In recent years, supporters at cricket matches have become much more active, forming supporters' clubs and even singing unofficial anthems. Groups such as England's 'Barmy Army' develop their own songs (most are too rude to reproduce here) and styles of banter, which is usually pretty good humoured. One of the most popular anthems (sung to the tune of Lord of the Dance) goes like this:

'Sing, sing wherever you may be
We are the famous Barmy Army
And we'll cheer England on, wherever they may be
And we'll sing them on to another victory'

- **Milestones.** The batting and fielding teams should acknowledge milestones for a batsman – 50, 100, and so on – with polite applause. A bowler who has taken five or more wickets should be allowed to lead his team from the field of play at the end.

Pocket Fact

When the legendary Australian batsman Don Bradman came out for his final innings in test cricket, at the Oval, London in 1948, he was given three cheers at the wicket by the England fielders. Unfortunately for Bradman, he scored 0.

- **After the game.** The batting team's players should walk onto the outfield and applaud the fielding team and the batsmen as they come off at the end. The fielding team should return the applause and the captains (or the whole of both teams) should shake hands.

The order of play

A day's cricket varies depending on the form of the game being played, and is only formally agreed on a series-by-series basis by the governing bodies of both teams. But at test match level, the structure of the day is fairly well set in two-hour slots. In England, this normally equates to the following schedule:

- *11am–1pm first session*
- *1pm–1.40pm lunch interval*
- *1.40pm–3.40pm second session*
- *3.40pm–4pm tea interval*
- *4pm–6pm final session*

In addition:

- *The final session of play in a test match can be extended by 30 minutes if there haven't been enough overs bowled in the three sessions.*
- *If an innings ends close to a scheduled break, that break may be taken early.*
- *If the batting team has lost nine wickets by the time of the tea break, the break can be delayed by 30 minutes or until the last wicket has fallen, whichever is sooner.*
- *There are five-minute breaks every hour of play for drinks.*
- *There is a 10-minute break between innings.*

● WHAT'S FOR TEA? THE ●
ETIQUETTE OF FOOD

If anything is critical to the overall success of a cricket match it's the food that you eat at tea. A limp tuna sandwich and cup of insipid orange squash is the final straw for many amateur cricketers, especially those who imagined cricket teas would consist of delicate cucumber sandwiches, an array of cakes and pastries, copious tea served in china cups and maybe a glass of ale to wash it down with the strawberries and cream for pudding.

The reality is that cricket lunches and teas fall into two categories: the professional and the amateur.

Professional lunches and teas

These are more about getting the right levels of nutrition and energy into the players:

- Lunch will consist of a main meal such as pasta, curry and rice, stir-fried vegetables, chicken or fish and potatoes, along with soup and bread.

- Players who are fielding immediately after lunch will often eat a lighter meal.

- Tea will consist of sandwiches, muffins, fruit and energy bars.

Pocket Fact ✐

The cricket tea has evolved from the fact that the earliest games involved a great deal of feasting on the part of the spectators: tents would be erected for the ladies (and a separate one for the gentlemen) to take tea while the game was in progress. It's no surprise that the players decided to get in on the act.

Amateur lunches and teas

These are more about buying the cheapest possible ingredients to fill up 22 hungry players in the shortest possible time:

- Tea will often consist of sandwiches – usually cheese, ham or tuna – on white bread, cake, crisps, sausage rolls and tea or squash.

- Big pot meals are also popular tea-time alternatives – rice and peas or a large chicken curry with bread will suffice for both teams.

- Players who are fielding after tea will often feel bloated and full of regret!

Pocket Fact

When Australian spinner Shane Warne toured India in 1998, he found the local curries weren't to his taste, so he requested a shipment of his favourite foods – baked beans and tinned spaghetti – be sent out to the tour party. Manufacturer Heinz responded by sending 2,000 cans to Warne.

● IT'S JUST NOT CRICKET ●

THE TOP TEN EXAMPLES OF BAD CONDUCT BY CRICKETERS

The more a game matters to people, the more they will do to try and secure a victory at all costs. But sometimes this has led to extraordinary lapses in judgement, as these examples show:

1. **Chappell's underarm tactics.** In the final over of a one-day match between Australia and New Zealand in 1981, New Zealand required six runs from the final ball to tie the match. Australia captain Greg Chappell instructed the bowler, his brother Trevor, to bowl the ball underarm along the ground, thus making a six impossible. It was within the laws (although they were subsequently amended to outlaw it) but both men were roundly booed by the crowd and criticised by almost everyone else.

2. **No-go Bravo.** In a Champions Trophy game for West Indies against England, bowler Dwayne Bravo claimed he had taken a

catch to dismiss batsman Michael Yardy when replays showed the ball clearly hit the ground in front of the fielder first. Bravo was charged with 'failing to conduct play within the spirit of the game' but was not banned.

3. **Singh slings his hook.** In the first series of the Indian Premier League competition, Indian bowler Harbhajan Singh slapped the face of an opponent, Sreesanth. Harbhajan claimed he was angered by Sreesanth's aggressive manner when celebrating the fall of wickets.

4. **Broad side.** England opening batsman Chris Broad was known for having a fiery temperament. When he was dismissed at the 1988 Sydney Bicentennial test match, he turned around and smashed the stumps out of the ground with his bat.

5. **Broad side (the next generation).** Chris' son Stuart has inherited the skills and the temperament of his father. In the test series against Pakistan in 2010, Broad became frustrated by the defensive play of debutant batsman Zulqarnain Haider, and after one defensive stroke, Broad picked up the ball and threw it at the batsman, hitting his hand. Broad was fined for the incident.

6. **Nel's raspberry.** In December 2003, South African pace bowler Andre Nel dismissed a West Indies opener and then stuck out his tongue at the batsman as he was departing. He was fined for his conduct.

7. **Lillee v Miandad.** Two of the game's most outspoken players squared up to each other at the WACA in Australia in 1981, when Miandad, running a single, collided with Lillee. The batsman claimed Lillee had blocked his path, kicking him in the process, and the bowler said Miandad had hit him with his bat. In the mêlée, Miandad nearly did hit Lillee with the bat but umpire Tony Crafter intervened. Both players were banned for two games.

8. **Inzamam's crowd trouble.** While fielding in an exhibition match against India in Toronto, Canada in 1997, Pakistan's

Inzamam-ul-Haq, a cricketer famous for being a larger gentleman but also extremely mild-mannered, responded to the taunts of a spectator by grabbing a bat and climbing into the stands intent on clubbing the offender. He was stopped, and although local police investigated the incident, no charges were brought on either side.

9. **Rose's thorny issue.** In 1979, Brian Rose, captain of Somerset in England, worked out that by declaring his team's innings closed after one over he would ensure they qualified for the quarter finals of the Benson and Hedges Cup competition. Their opponents Worcestershire took 10 balls to score the two runs required to win the game and both teams qualified. It was unorthodox, but within the law. It didn't impress the cricket authorities, who threw Somerset out of the competition.

10. **Sunny spits dummy.** In 1981, India's Sunil Gavaskar was batting against Australia at Melbourne when he was given out leg before wicket (lbw) by rookie test umpire Rex Whitehead. Gavaskar insisted that he'd hit the ball and was very reluctant to leave the field. Bowler Dennis Lillee remonstrated until Gavaskar took offence at Lillee's tone and tried to persuade his batting partner Chetan Chauhan to follow him off – which would have forfeited the match. Chauhan went with him, but was stopped on the boundary edge by the Indian team manager and persuaded to return and continue his innings.

Pocket Fact

Australian post-war fast bowler Keith Miller was well known for his slick 'Brylcreemed' hair, but this was his secret weapon too – before bowling he would pass his hand through his hair and apply a discreet coating of hair cream to the shiny side of the ball.

6

THE MAIN FORMS OF THE GAME

Cricket is basically baseball on valium.
Robin Williams

Though it's an eye-catching quote, Robin Williams's comment ignores something fundamental – cricket isn't simply one thing, by any means. It's a whole set of different disciplines which require very different approaches from the players. Here we look at the different forms of the game – from the ultimate test of five-day cricket to the not-so-humble grass roots of the amateur game.

⚉ TEST CRICKET ⚉

BASICS

Test cricket is defined as a game lasting a maximum of five days played by two of the 10 test-playing nations recognised by the ICC:

- Australia

- Bangladesh

- England

- India

- New Zealand

- Pakistan

- South Africa

- Sri Lanka

- West Indies

- Zimbabwe

Each day's play is about six hours – or 90 overs – in length.

Each team has two innings, each of which can only be ended when all the batsmen are out, when the five days have elapsed, or when the captain of the batting side declares his team's innings closed. If the fourth innings of the game – or even an earlier innings – is still being played at the end of the fifth day's play, the match is drawn.

AIM OF THE GAME

Although every test match depends on the fine details of weather, pitch condition and player fitness, the essential goals remain pretty consistent. There are two basic scenarios:

1. **Team A win the toss and bat first.** Team A build up a good first innings total – essential for applying pressure later in the game. On a good batting wicket, teams should be scoring between 100 and 120 runs per two-hour session of play, so providing there's no dramatic loss of wickets, Team A should have a decent total – 400 runs or more – by lunch on the second day. The pressure is then on Team B to score the same or better, and this can often lead to mistakes. If they score just 300 runs, Team A have a lead of 100 going into the second innings. A second innings total of 250-plus will make the victory target of 350 almost impossible for Team B and Team A normally bowl out the opposition to win by the number of runs by which Team B have fallen short.

2. **Team A win the toss and field first.** If the wicket, or the weather, suggest that the conditions favour bowling then Team A may choose to make Team B bat in the hope that they can get them all out for a low total (150, for example). Then, when the conditions change later in the game, Team A can bat, build a good first innings lead (with a score of 350, say) and apply pressure in the second innings. Team B must score at least 200 to avoid an innings defeat, but if they make only 250, which is a fairly typical second innings total, they leave Team A the

target of just 51 runs to win. If Team A lose just one wicket while doing this, they win by nine wickets.

Of course, there are many variations on the above, but these scenarios tell us two essential things – firstly that winning the toss can make a huge difference in cricket, and secondly that the balance of power in a game lasting five days can swing from one side to the other depending on a dizzying variety of internal and external factors. That's what makes test cricket such an absorbing game.

History

When England met Australia at Melbourne over four days in March 1877, test cricket was born, but it didn't completely resemble the game played today. It wasn't even known as 'test' cricket until the end of the 19th century. Here are some of the other key points of evolution.

Test cricket and international cricket

We need to make a distinction here between test and international cricket. Though it seems elitist, tests can only be played between the above-mentioned teams, so the first 'official' international game was the one played between Australia and England in 1877.

The first international cricket match actually happened more than 30 years previously, in 1844, when the USA met Canada in Manhattan. It was a heavily publicised event which attracted a lot of spectators and a huge number of bets were placed on the outcome. It was a low-scoring single-innings game which Canada won. Rematches were played in the years that followed, but the game of cricket was almost completely wiped out in the USA by the civil war.

The USA and Canada met in 2004 for an ICC trophy limited overs game – the first 'first-class' cricket match between the nations 160 years after their first meeting.

- **Duration.** The first games were played over three or four days, but often the final test match in a series was left open – as a so-called 'timeless' test. The last of these was played between England and South Africa in 1939 and went on for nine days, with England only abandoning their second innings run-chase (at 654–5, the highest fourth innings total ever made) because they would have missed the boat home if they'd carried on. After the Second World War test matches were limited to five days.

- **Frequency.** In the early days of test match cricket a touring team was made up of whoever was available to spend six months out of the country travelling and playing. As most cricketers were amateurs, many players were prevented from touring by work. The number of test matches in a series is agreed by the governing bodies of the teams taking part and depends on other commitments, but most international teams play around 10 to 12 tests per year on average – six or seven at home and five or six abroad.

- **Politics.** The list of test-playing nations has been affected by national politics over the years. In 1970, South Africa were banned from playing test cricket because of the government's apartheid policy (they were restored in 1991). In recent times, a variety of nations, including England, New Zealand and Australia have refused to play matches against Zimbabwe, although Zimbabwe still have test-playing status. Due to security fears and natural disasters, the Pakistan team were unable to play home fixtures in 2010, and instead played their 'summer' games in England.

Pocket Fact

Cricket has always been a statistician's game, but the development of the ICC's Test Match Championship allows test-playing teams to be ranked in a table depending on their results. Set up in 2001, the table was dominated by Australia for the early part of its first decade, but a variety of teams have held the title of 'number one', including India and South Africa.

● DOMESTIC (FIRST-CLASS) ● CRICKET

BASICS

Domestic cricket is the name given to the competitions played over three to five days with two innings per side that many leading cricketing nations operate. In England this is the County Championship, in Australia it is the Sheffield Shield, and in India it is the Ranji Trophy. Forms of the game and tournaments come and go, but essentially this kind of game is played according to the same laws and with the same kinds of kit as test match cricket. As the games are often shorter than test matches there is a higher percentage of draws, but these games are seen as a valuable 'proving ground' for future international players.

HISTORY

It's difficult to accurately date domestic cricket, as teams claiming to represent the states of India or Australia and the counties of England have played against each other since the game first became popular. But there are official dates of the first seasons in each of the major tournaments around the world:

- **1889:** Currie Cup (South Africa – now SuperSport Series)

- **1890:** County Championship (England – a two-tier system since 2000)

- **1892:** Sheffield Shield (Australia)

- **1903:** Logan Cup (Zimbabwe – first-class since 1992)

- **1906:** Plunket Shield (New Zealand – played as a league since 1921)

- **1934:** Ranji Trophy (India)

- **1938:** Daily News Trophy (Sri Lanka – now Premier Trophy)

- **1965:** Shell Shield (West Indies – now Regional Four Day Competition)

⚫ ONE-DAY (LIMITED OVERS) ⚫ CRICKET

BASICS

As the name suggests, one-day cricket is a game that should be completed in a single day's play. Major games like internationals or cup finals often have a second day reserved for play if weather leads to the abandonment of the game.

One-day cricket has both domestic and international forms, which have slightly different structures.

The domestic game

The domestic game around the world has a variety of tournaments and leagues. The first was called the Gillette Cup, which started in England in 1963. Games can be played over 40, 50 or 60 overs a side. Games must produce a result, and so there are no draws in limited overs cricket. However, if the teams have identical scores after the allocated overs have been bowled the game is called a tie and the points (if it is a league or cup game) are shared. In rain-affected games, the result is often calculated using the Duckworth – Lewis method of scoring (see p. 25).

The international game

One-day internationals began in January 1971 with a game between Australia and England at Melbourne (the scene of much of cricket's innovation). Games are standardised at 50 overs per side. In addition to the 10 test playing teams, the following are recognised as 'official' one-day international teams by the ICC:

- Afghanistan

- Canada

- Ireland

- Kenya

- Netherlands

- Scotland

On an international level, one-day cricket tournaments are usually played between teams as part of a tour that includes test matches, or as part of a specific knockout tournament such as the ICC Champions Trophy or the World Cup (see Chapter 8).

Whether it's played nationally or internationally, limited overs cricket has some unique features that don't apply in other forms of the game. These include the following:

Limited bowling

Bowlers are limited to a maximum number of overs in a game. In a 50-over international, no bowler can bowl more than 10 overs.

Fielding restrictions

These restrict the number of players permitted in the outfield during the first 10 overs of an innings to two. These restrictions come into force for a further two sessions of five overs each, one decided by the captain of the batting side and the other by the captain of the fielding side. These are known as 'power plays'. At other times, the fielding side is permitted a maximum of five fielders in the outfield.

Timing

The fast and furious nature of one-day cricket means it is more likely to adapt to innovation than its serious older brother, the test match. So it has become common to experiment with day/night games which begin at 2pm and continue until nightfall under floodlights.

Dress

The brightly coloured pyjama kits of each state, county, province or nation are an expression of individuality.

Ball

The ball is white so that it can be seen against the colourful clothing, but also in the fading light of a day/night match.

Name

Especially true in domestic competitions, each team selects a nickname to append to its official title, so for example, the county of Kent becomes the Kent Spitfires in the one-day game.

Pocket Fact ✎

Not all innovations in cricket turn out to be entirely successful. In 2005, the ICC trialled a scheme called 'super sub' in which each team nominated at the toss a substitute who would be able to bat, bowl or field, who would replace a colleague at any stage in the game for the remainder of the game. After a few months of extremely reluctant trial, the scheme was dropped as it seemed to favour the team winning the toss.

⦿ TWENTY20 (T20) CRICKET ⦿

BASICS

A shortened form of limited overs cricket, Twenty20 owes much to the one-day game in terms of structure and rules – limited number of overs per bowler, field restrictions, plenty of razzmatazz – but it is an even more concentrated and exciting game that relies much more on powerful and ingenious batting and accurate, frustrating bowling. The game is played over a period of approximately three hours, with 20 overs per side. Teams rarely exceed a total of 200 runs in an innings, with the average being around the 130–150 mark. There are national Twenty20 tournaments all over the world – some of which have become massive industries (see Indian Premier League box below) – as well as international matches and tournaments.

HISTORY

The first Twenty20 games were played in England in 2003 after the England and Wales Cricket Board (ECB) devised the format to replace a defunct one-day cup competition. Although the format is young, it has experienced rapid growth. Here's a brief timeline of key events:

- **2003:** First T20 Cup held in England and won by the Surrey Lions.

- **2004:** T20 Cup match held at Lord's for the first time.

- **2005 (January):** First T20 game in Australia.

- **2005 (February):** First international T20 game played between Australia and New Zealand in Auckland.

- **2006:** Stanford 20–20 cup competition launched in West Indies.

- **2007:** First T20 World Cup held in South Africa and won by India.

- **2008:** First season of Indian Premier League.

- **2009:** Second T20 World Cup held in England and won by Pakistan.

- **2010:** Third T20 World Cup held in West Indies and won by England.

Indian Premier League – a runaway success

The Indian Premier League (IPL) is the epitome of T20's ambition. It is a lively, incredibly exciting tournament which uses the best players from throughout India and the world. Many of the world's greatest cricketers have played in the IPL – some have even retired from other forms of the game to concentrate on their IPL career. But it's a tournament that's had its fair share of ups and downs in its short history – with betting rife in the game and extraordinary sums being paid out to secure the services of the star players like Shane Warne, Adam Gilchrist, Andrew Flintoff and Sachin Tendulkar.

In 2009, the entire tournament was moved to South Africa at just three weeks' notice to ensure the safety of players and spectators alike following terrorist attacks in Mumbai.

REGULATIONS

T20 is similar to the one-day game, but there are some specific rules that apply only to this form of the game:

- Bowlers can only bowl a maximum of four overs.

- A no-ball in T20 costs the bowling side a one-run penalty as in other forms of the game but it is also followed by a 'free hit' – an extra ball which the batsman can only get out from if he is run out, hits the ball twice, obstructs the field or handles the ball.

- Only five fielders are allowed on the leg side.

- During the first six overs, only two fielders are allowed in the outfield.

● WOMEN'S CRICKET ●

Women have played cricket since the very early days of the game, but it is only over the last 10 to 15 years that the game has enjoyed a really serious rise in profile and popularity, due mainly to a change in the way the game was promoted throughout the world. Here's a brief timeline of significant dates in the women's game:

- **1745:** First recorded women-only game (Hambledon v Bramley).

- **1887:** First women's club is formed, in Yorkshire, England.

- **1890s:** Women's cricket leagues are established in Australia and South Africa.

- **1926:** English Women's Cricket Association (WCA) is formed to oversee women's game in England.

- **1958:** International Women's Cricket Council (IWCC) is formed to organise and oversee international fixtures.

- **1998:** WCA merges with the England and Wales Cricket Board (ECB).

- **2005:** IWCC merges with ICC.

- **2009:** Claire Taylor of England named as one of Wisden Cricketers of the Year.

- **2009:** ICC Women's Cricket World Cup staged – England win.

- **2010 (August):** Former England captain Rachel Heyhoe-Flint inducted into the ICC Hall of Fame.

While the women's game may not be as fast and as physical as the men's version, there is every indication that, with the ICC's strength behind the game internationally, women's cricket is set to grow hugely in the coming years.

> *Pocket Fact* ✐
>
> *Central contracts for international players have been a contentious issue in the men's game (see p. 121), but in the women's game, national cricket boards pay these retainers to a core of leading players which allows them to focus on their cricket and is one of the main reasons for the resurgence of the game. England, West Indies and Pakistan all have strong central contracts policies.*

● DISABILITY CRICKET ●

Cricket for people with disabilities – whether physically disabled, visually impaired or with learning difficulties – is another burgeoning area of the game. In England, the ECB (England and Wales Cricket Board) has appointed a full-time officer to oversee the growth of disability cricket and many of the English counties have disability cricket coaching sessions and specific courses.

Internationally, matches have been played in India, Sri Lanka and South Africa, with most of the leading test-playing nations fielding disability cricket teams.

● AMATEUR CRICKET ●

Last, but certainly not least, on the scale of organised cricket is the grassroots game – whether it be local league cricket, village cricket, school competitions or just a group of friends on tour, the amateur form of the game is truly the lifeblood of every other element.

Here are just some of the reasons why this form of the game has contributed so much to the longevity and success of cricket in general.

It is inclusive

In amateur cricket the age range in a side may span 50 years or more and the level of ability may have a similarly wide spread. Players are chosen not just for their skills but for other qualities such as reliability, usefulness (they have a big car to carry the team's kit or they run the local pub) and determination (they are prepared to spend hours chasing up all the other players to get a team together each week). The last evening league game I played was for a team that included two teenagers, a 60-year-old and two brilliantly talented women. What other game allows such an inclusive team line-up?

It is social

The rituals of amateur cricket mean that it's a whole-day activity. In a weekend game, the ritual begins at midday, with a meeting in the pub and a drink to catch up on the week's news. The team then go to the ground, inspect the pitch, play the game and return to the pub to celebrate or to drown sorrows. All of this takes approximately 12 hours out of the day. What better way to reduce the stress of a hectic working schedule than to have an enforced day-long focus on playing games?

It is innovative

The ECB (England and Wales Cricket Board) is very proud of having developed Twenty20 – a competition that is hugely successful. In truth, Twenty20 is just a professional version of the game that evening cricketers have been playing for decades – 20 overs a side, four overs per bowler and as many runs as possible in whatever way you can get them. Ok, so there weren't any cheerleaders and fireworks, but evening cricket must lay claim to being the original exciting short form of the game.

It is simple

Without the constraints of league rules, most truly amateur sides don't have to worry too much about the condition of their kit or whether they've got two recognised umpires. As long as there's a pitch, a bat and a ball, there's a game of cricket in the offing.

It builds bridges

If the social aspect of the weekend cricketer appeals to you, try getting involved with a team that tours. The amateur tour is a focused excuse to socialise with people in another part of the country – perhaps even another part of the world. Ditchling Cricket Club, a village side from Sussex in England, even went as far as Afghanistan in 2009 to play a game against the Afghan national team. Many teams have a charitable focus to their tours.

Pocket Fact

The sheer joy of amateur cricket is captured brilliantly in literature. Some of the great books on the subject are The Cricket Match *by Hugh de Selincourt,* The Village Cricket Tour *by Vernon Coleman and* Many a Slip *by Gideon Haigh.*

7

THE TEAMS

In the end it is only the camaraderie of the team, the lifelong friendships which you forge . . . which make the experience worthwhile.
Bill O'Reilly

All the laws in the world, manicured pitches and beautifully designed stadia, wouldn't count for very much without two teams of 11 to fight each other for the honour of claiming victory. Cricket has been played at the highest level for more than 130 years, but it has been the preserve of relatively few teams. Now though, thanks in large part to the ambition of the ICC, the game has become truly worldwide. In this chapter we take a closer look at the leading test-playing nations and also at the lower-profile teams that are hoping to change the face of cricket in the future.

● THE TEST-PLAYING NATIONS ●
(ICC FULL MEMBERS)

WHAT IS ICC FULL MEMBERSHIP?

Full membership of the ICC permits teams to play test matches, one day internationals and Twenty20 internationals. Full members also automatically pre-qualify for the World Cup and Twenty20 World Cup tournaments. The actual members of the ICC are the governing bodies of the test playing nations, the teams themselves are the playing representatives of their respective governing bodies.

AUSTRALIA

First test match
1877 v England at Melbourne.

First one-day international
1971 v England at Melbourne.

Colours
Green and gold. The players wear a distinctive green cap known as 'the baggy green'.

History
As the joint oldest test-playing nation, Australia have a cricketing history spanning the game's international status. In recent years Australia have completely dominated world cricket, spending many years as the number one nation in the ICC ranking of test and one-day international matches. Although the country's dominance of cricket has started to fade, there is still no doubt that a game against Australia represents a massive challenge for any other side. The long history of Ashes tests (see p. 116), which began in 1882, are still widely regarded as one of the most important clashes in any sport.

Honours
- Winners of the Cricket World Cup in 1987, 1999, 2003, 2007.
- Runners-up in 1975 and 1996.
- Winners of the Champions Trophy in 2006 and 2009.
- Runners-up World Twenty20 Cup in 2010.

Great players
Australia have given the world so many great players just a selection can be mentioned here, but the all-time greats list would certainly include:

- Fred Spofforth (test career 1877–1887)
- Keith Miller (1945–1957)
- Victor Trumper (1899–1912)
- Ray Lindwall (1945–1960)
- Bill Ponsford (1924–1934)
- Neil Harvey (1947–1963)
- Don Bradman (1928–1948)
- Richie Benaud (1951–1964)

- Rod Marsh
  (1970–1984)

- Dennis Lillee (1970–1984)

- Allan Border (1978–1994)

- Steve Waugh (1985–2004)

- Glenn McGrath
  (1993–2007)

- Shane Warne (1991–2007)

- Adam Gilchrist (1999–2008)

- Ricky Ponting (1995–)

Pocket Fact

Australian cricketers have a pathological fear of the score 87 – known as 'the devil's number' – as it is 13 runs short of a century. It's regarded as being a dangerous score to stay on for any time, which perhaps explains why so many batsmen get out on 87 as they make poor shot choices to escape the curse.

BANGLADESH

First test match
2000 v India at Dhaka.

First one-day international
1986 v Pakistan, Asia Cup.

Colours
Green. The team are nicknamed 'The Tigers'.

History
The nation of Bangladesh gained independence in 1971. They are the most recent test match playing nation and have worked hard to shake off the reputation of minnows, particularly in the one-day form of the game, where they have managed to beat all of the other nations. In test matches the team's record is not so impressive, but the country has made great strides in just a decade of playing cricket at the highest level.

Honours
The greatest moments of Bangladeshi cricket to date are the victory over Pakistan in the 1999 World Cup, which put the team

on the map, the team's first test match victory against Zimbabwe in January 2005, and a one-day series win against New Zealand in October 2010.

Great players

- Mashrafe Mortaza (test career 2001–2009)

- Mohammed Ashraful (2001–)

- Mohammed Rafique (2001–2008)

- Tamim Iqbal (2007–)

- Shakib Al Hasan (2007–)

Pocket Fact

Cricket writer Robin Marlar took up the cause of Bangladesh cricket in 1976, when he wrote an impassioned article in The International Cricketer *magazine, imploring the game's authorities to support and recognise Bangladesh's status. An MCC side toured the country soon after, although official recognition was still almost 25 years away.*

ENGLAND

First test match
1877 v Australia at Melbourne.

First one-day international
1971 v Australia at Melbourne.

Colours
Red and blue. The players wear a navy-blue cap.

History
England share the longevity honours with Australia, but are still quite a long way behind in terms of overall number of test match victories. The rivalries with Australia in the Ashes contests and with West Indies are the most eagerly anticipated by the English cricket supporters, but the game in England is no longer

held in the same regard as it is in countries like India and Pakistan. It is still extremely popular in England, and the team are widely supported, but recent innovations like Twenty20 cricket have proved more successful as spectator sports than the traditional domestic County Championship. The test match side have enjoyed a resurgence in recent years, with notable Ashes victories in England in 2005 and 2009, though these two series victories sat either side of a 5–0 whitewash at the hands of the Australians in 2006–2007. In 2010–2011, England beat the Australians in Australia for the first time in 24 years – taking the series 3–1 and subsequently retaining the Ashes for the first time in a quarter of a century as well.

Honours

- Winners of World Twenty20 Cup in 2010

- Runners-up in Cricket World Cup in 1975, 1987 and 1992

- Runners-up in Champions Trophy in 2004

Great players

- WG Grace (test career 1880–1899)

- Jack Hobbs (1907–1930)

- Wilfred Rhodes (1899–1930)

- Harold Larwood (1926–1933)

- Herbert Sutcliffe (1924–1935)

- Alec Bedser (1946–1955)

- Denis Compton (1937–1957)

- Len Hutton (1937–1955)

- Jim Laker (1947–1959)

- Peter May (1951–1961)

- Brian Statham (1950–1965)

- Fred Trueman (1952–1965)

- Colin Cowdrey (1954–1975)

- Alan Knott (1967–1981)

- Geoffrey Boycott (1964–1982)

- Ian Botham (1977–1992)

- David Gower (1978–1992)

- Graham Gooch (1975–1995)

Pocket Fact

As with Australia's fear of the number 87, English cricketers are often concerned when the score reaches 111 as this score looks like the three stumps without bails, a sure sign that a wicket is going to be lost. It is known as a Nelson, after the war hero Horatio Nelson who was wrongly believed to have one eye, one arm and one leg.

INDIA

First test match
1932 v England at Lord's.

First one-day international
1974 v England at Headingley.

Colours
Orange and blue.

History
The history of Indian cricket is closely allied to the history of India. It was dominated by the presence of the English until the first half of the 20th century, and it has steadily grown in prominence. Cricket was first played in India way back in 1721, when it was introduced by English sailors. One of the greatest sporting clubs in the world, the Calcutta Cricket Club, was founded in 1792, but the national team didn't play any test matches until 1932, when a touring side visited England. Prior to that, leading India stars like Ranjitsinhji and Duleepsinhji were drafted into the England cricket team with great success.

India's first test match victory was in 1952 and this was a turning point, with the Indian team growing in strength and prominence thanks largely to a brilliant spin bowling attack and some tenacious batsmen, including two of the world's finest – Gavaskar and Tendulkar. By 2010 India had risen to the rank of number one in the ICC Test Rankings.

Honours

- Winners of Cricket World Cup in 1983
- Runners-up in Champions Trophy in 2000
- Winners of Twenty20 World Cup in 2007

Great players

- CK Nayudu (test career 1932–1936)
- Vijay Merchant (1933–1952)
- Vinoo Mankad (1946–1959)
- Nawab of Pataudi (1961–1975)
- Bhagwat Candrasekhar (1963–1979)
- Bishan Bedi (1966–1979)
- Sunil Gavaskar (1970–1987)
- Kapil Dev (1978–1994)
- Mohammad Azharuddin (1984–2000)
- Sourav Ganguly (1996–2009)
- Anil Kumble (1990–2009)
- Rahul Dravid (1996–)
- Sachin Tendulkar (1989–)

Pocket Fact

Nari Contractor, captain of the Indian cricket team in the early 1960s, was struck on the back of the skull by a ball from West Indian pace bowler Charlie Griffith which left him unconscious and gravely ill for six days. Following emergency surgery his life was saved and he was back playing first-class cricket within two years. This remains the most serious injury to a professional cricketer to date.

NEW ZEALAND

First test match
1930 v England at Christchurch.

First one-day international
1973 v Pakistan at Christchurch.

Colours
Black.

History
New Zealand might be a relative newcomer to the test match arena, but the history of cricket in the country goes back a very long way. When Charles Darwin visited the island in 1835, he noted a cricket match being played by freed slaves. The national team though were not to play at the highest level for almost 100 years, and the early days of test match cricket were quite a challenge. From the 1960s to the 1980s, however, New Zealand grew steadily as a force in world cricket, thanks largely to the batting of John Reid, Martin Crowe and Glenn Turner and the all-round heroics of Richard Hadlee. The high point of this era came in 1985, in a test match against the Australians at Brisbane, when Hadlee took 15 wickets in the match (including 9–52 in the Australian first innings) and Crowe scored 188. The New Zealanders won by an innings. Since the 1990s, New Zealand have struggled to compete with the strongest nations in test matches, but have continued to prosper in the one-day game.

Honours
Runners-up in Champions Trophy of 2009.

Great players
- Bert Sutcliffe (test career 1946–1965)
- John R. Reid (1949–1965)
- Glenn Turner (1968–1983)
- Jeremy Coney (1973–1987)
- Richard Hadlee (1972–1990)
- Ian Smith (1980–1992)
- Martin Crowe (1981–1996)
- Chris Cairns (1989–2004)
- Nathan Astle (1995–2007)
- Stephen Fleming (1993–2008)
- Shane Bond (2001–2010)
- Daniel Vettori (1996–)

Pocket Fact

New Zealand played Australia in the first international Twenty20 game – at Auckland in 2005. The game was played in a very light-hearted manner to put to rest the simmering anger of the famous underarm bowling incident of 1981 (see p. 71). Players wore 1980s fancy dress and Aussie bowler Glenn McGrath was shown a football red card by umpire Billy Bowden for bowling a joke underarm delivery.

PAKISTAN

First test match
1952 v India at Delhi.

First one-day international
1973 v New Zealand at Christchurch.

Colours
Green and gold.

History
Cricket in Pakistan is a huge and passionate industry, but the national side are frustratingly inconsistent, typified by some extraordinary talents yet also cursed with a talent to implode at the wrong moment. On the plus side, Pakistani bowlers have introduced the world to incredible forms of artistry – notably the reverse swing bowling of Imran Khan, Waqar Younis and Wasim Akram in the 1980s and 1990s. Batsmen of the quality of Javed Miandad and Zaheer Abbas pushed Pakistan's cause to be regarded as a major force in world cricket. But misfortunes such as the unfounded allegations of ball-tampering that led to the forfeit of a test match in England in 2006, the team's shock exit from the World Cup in 2007 at the hands of Ireland and the spot-fixing allegations that blighted the team's tour in England in 2010 all contribute to a patchy record that is below the standard required by the team's legions of adoring fans.

Honours

- Winners of 2009 World Twenty20 Cup
- Runners-up in 2007 World Twenty20 Cup
- Winners of 1996 World Cup
- Runners-up in 1999 World Cup

Great players

- Hanif Mohammad (test career 1952–1970)
- Zaheer Abbas (1969–1986)
- Abdul Qadir (1977–1991)
- Imran Khan (1971–1992)
- Javed Miandad (1976–1994)
- Rashid Latif (1992–2003)
- Wasim Akram (1984–2002)
- Waqar Younis (1989–2003)
- Mushtaq Ahmed (1989–2004)
- Saqlain Mushtaq (1995–2004)
- Inzamam-ul-Haq (1992–2008)
- Danish Kaneria (2000–2010)

Pocket Fact

In 1958 Pakistan opening batsman Hanif Mohammad set a unique record – his 337 runs were scored in 970 minutes making it the slowest triple-century ever scored and the longest innings by any batsman in international cricket. He was at the wicket for around three days.

SOUTH AFRICA

First test match
1889 v England at Port Elizabeth.

First one-day international
1991 v India at Calcutta.

Colours
Green and gold.

History

A bit like India, South Africa has a cricketing history that is inseparable from its political history. It is a story of two halves. The first half is South Africa as a pioneering nation of cricket, one of the founder members of the ICC and a major force in the development of world cricket. Great players like Dudley Nourse helped South Africa keep pace with England and Australia in the first half of the 20th century. The team improved still further in the postwar period and were close to their best with players like Graeme Pollock and Barry Richards emerging in the late 1960s when the ICC decided to ban the South Africans from international cricket as a response to apartheid. The ban was to last 21 years – the entirety of the careers of some great players, and when the team did return in the 1990s, they took some time to become established as a leading force again. But by the beginning of the 21st century, South African cricket was in the safe hands of captain Graeme Smith and riding high in the world rankings. All that remains is to convert the team's all-round dominance into trophy-winning performances.

Honours

Winners (gold medallists) Commonwealth Games cricket tournament 1998.

Great players

- Aubrey Faulkner (test career 1905–1924)
- Dudley Nourse (1935–1951)
- Mike Procter (1966–1970)
- Graeme Pollock (1963–1970)
- Barry Richards (1969–1970)
- Peter Kirsten (1991–1994)
- Hansie Cronje (1991–2000)
- Jonty Rhodes (1992–2000)
- Allan Donald (1991–2002)
- Gary Kirsten (1993–2004)
- Shaun Pollock (1995–2008)
- Jacques Kallis (1995–)
- Graeme Smith (2001–)
- Mark Boucher (1997–)

Pocket Fact

South Africa have developed a reputation for being the nearly-men of international cricket. They have reached the semi-finals in ICC international competitions no fewer than six times since 1992 but have never yet appeared in a final.

SRI LANKA

First test match
1982 v England at Colombo.

First one-day international
1982 v England at Colombo (first played in World Cup 1975).

Colours
Dark blue, gold and red.

History
Sri Lanka's rise to prominence in international cricket has been nothing short of meteoric. Although the Sri Lankans (as Ceylon) played first-class cricket as far back as 1926, the team were not granted test status until the 1980s, but wasted no time becoming a leading force. With the bowling of greats like Muralitharan and Vaas, and the batting of Jayasuriya among others, Sri Lanka have become famous as a free-scoring team well-known for attractive cricket and open games. The Sri Lankans' success rate in ICC competition is remarkable – they genuinely give the impression of being a team with nothing to fear who have become incredibly hard to beat.

Honours
- Runners-up in 2009 World Twenty20 Cup
- Winners of 1996 World Cup
- Runners-up in 2007 World Cup
- Winners of 2002 Champions Trophy

Great players

- Arjuna Ranatunga (test career 1981–2000)
- Aravinda de Silva (1984–2002)
- Marvan Atapattu (1990–2008)
- Sanath Jayasuriya (1990–2008)
- Chaminda Vaas (1994–2009)
- Muttiah Muralitharan (1992–2010)
- Mahela Jayawardene (1997–)
- Kumar Sangakkara (2000–)

Pocket Fact

Sri Lanka are the only team to win the World Cup as hosts of the tournament.

WEST INDIES

First test match
1928 v England at Lord's.

First one-day international
1973 v England at Headingley.

Colours
Maroon and grey.

History
The West Indies entered the international arena as the fourth test-playing nation but in the early days they were still dominated by English ex-pats and the team's success was patchy. The real turning point came in the 1950s and 1960s when players like Gary Sobers, Wes Hall, Frank Worrell and Everton Weekes came through the ranks to establish the team's identity as a mixture of powerful stroke play and ferocious bowling. This reputation was further enhanced in the 1970s and 1980s when the fast bowling attack, spearheaded by players like Malcolm Marshall, became feared around the world for short-pitched bowling on hard surfaces.

Meanwhile, batsmen like Viv Richards were demonstrating the fearsome art of attacking batting that would make the West Indies the number one side in the world in the mid-1980s.

Although the team's fortunes have dipped in the past 20 years, they have continued to produce some of the world's greatest cricketers, most notably Brian Lara, who still holds the record for the highest score in test match cricket of 400 runs.

Honours
- Winners of 1975 World Cup
- Winners of 1979 World Cup
- Runners-up in 1983 World Cup
- Winners of 2004 Champions Trophy
- Runners-up in 1998 and 2006 Champions Trophy

Great players
- Learie Constantine (test career 1928–1939)
- George Headley (1929–1954)
- Everton Weekes (1947–1958)
- Frank Worrell (1947–1963)
- Wes Hall (1958–1969)
- Garfield (Gary) Sobers (1953–1974)
- Rohan Kanhai (1957–1974)
- Lance Gibbs (1957–1976)
- Clive Lloyd (1966–1985)
- Joel Garner (1976–1987)
- Michael Holding (1975–1987)
- Gordon Greenidge (1974–1991)
- Viv Richards (1974–1991)
- Malcolm Marshall (1978–1991)
- Desmond Haynes (1977–1994)
- Roger Harper (1983–1994)
- Courtney Walsh (1984–2001)
- Curtly Ambrose (1987–2000)
- Brian Lara (1990–2007)

Pocket Fact

From 1984 to 1985 West Indies won 11 test matches in a row – 10 of them against England in two separate 5–0 series wins. The West Indies fans dubbed these massive victories 'blackwashes'.

ZIMBABWE

First test match
1992 v India at Harare.

First one-day international
1992 v India at Harare (first played in 1983 World Cup).

Colours
Green, red and gold.

History
Zimbabwe are still new boys and they've had their fair share of teething problems. A slow start to test match cricket led to some criticisms that they were not good enough to compete at the top level, but a series of convincing one-day international displays changed public perception. Zimbabwe had a number of star players too – including Andy Flower and Heath Streak – who seemed to be bringing the young side into prominence. Unfortunately, politics intervened and a number of high-profile disputes between players and the Zimbabwean government led to strikes, protests and ultimately a self-imposed exile from test match cricket which came into force in 2006 and ended in 2011.

Honours
Winners of ICC Trophy in 1982, 1986, 1990.

Great players

- John Traicos (1970–1993)
- David Houghton (1992–1998)
- Henry Olonga (1994–2003)
- Andy Flower (1992–2003)
- Grant Flower (1992–2004)
- Mark Vermeulen (2002–2004)
- Heath Streak (1993–2006)
- Tatenda Taibu (2001–2006)

Pocket Fact

Zimbabwe share with India the indignity of being the only test match playing nations to be bowled out twice in the same day. For Zimbabwe, this miserable statistic came about in 2005, when they were beaten at home by New Zealand in a test match that lasted just two days.

● THE ONE-DAY INTERNATIONAL ● NATIONS (ICC ASSOCIATE MEMBERS)

WHAT IS ICC ASSOCIATE MEMBERSHIP?

ICC associate membership is given to governing bodies of nations which have established cricket leagues or where cricket is played on a regular basis. There are 35 associate members. The top six associate members based on performance in the World Cricket League are awarded one day international and Twenty20 international status. These teams are able to compete with full members in World Cup and Twenty20 World Cup tournaments.

AFGHANISTAN

Colours
Blue and red.

First one-day international
2009 v Scotland in South Africa.

History

Cricket was first played by English ex-pats in Afghanistan in the late 19th century, but it was only in 2000, when the ruling Taliban decided to allow the game to be played, that the foundations were laid for cricket's newest and fastest-growing international team. Although Afghanistan missed out on a place in the 2011 World Cup, a position of fifth in the qualifiers was enough to guarantee ODI status until 2013. The team did manage to qualify for the 2010 World Twenty20 Cup, but went out in the group stages.

Pocket Fact

Due to ongoing security concerns, Afghanistan played most of their early ODI games in Sharjah on the Arabian Gulf. An international standard cricket stadium has now been constructed in Nangarhar Province, Afghanistan. It opened to host matches in spring 2011.

CANADA

Colours
Red.

First one-day international
1979 v Pakistan at Headingley (World Cup).

History
As we've already seen, Canada have one of the longest records of any international cricket team, dating back to 1844 (see p. 77). But cricket has never been a major sport in the country even though Canada have made it into four World Cups and are one of the leading associate member nations. Star players like all-rounder John Davison (who played first-class cricket in Australia) have raised the profile of the Canadian game in recent years.

> ### Pocket Fact
>
> The Canadian side is a mixture of home-grown and ex-pat talent. In 2010, the team was made up of players born in a variety of places including three in Pakistan, two in India, two in Guyana, one in Uganda and three in Canada.

IRELAND

Colours
Black and green.

First one-day international
2006 v England at Belfast.

History
The first recorded game in Ireland was in 1855 and the Irish have played regular fixtures against touring sides as well as against England and Scotland since then. The game has always been amateur in Ireland, with the leading players often going to the English counties. Since the advent of one-day cricket, Ireland have steadily grown in stature and a great performance at the 2007 World Cup, in which they memorably beat Pakistan in the group stage, confirmed the nation's status as the next genuine contender for full ICC membership.

> ### Pocket Fact
>
> In 1969, a touring West Indies side – including the inspirational captain and batsman Clive Lloyd – were soundly thrashed by Ireland. The Irish bowled the visitors out for just 25 runs and won the game by nine wickets.

KENYA

Colours
Green, black and red.

First one-day international

1996 v India at Cuttack (World Cup).

History

Kenya have long been regarded as the strongest associate team in Africa. For a time they played their games in partnership with Uganda and Tanzania under the banner of East Africa, with this team winning a place at the first World Cup in 1975. In 1981, Kenya split from the other countries and were given their own ICC associate membership. More World Cup success followed, with major upsets, such as a convincing win over the West Indies in 1996 and an extraordinary semi-final appearance in 2003.

Pocket Fact

Kenya's greatest player to date is all-rounder Steve Tikolo, who has amassed more than 3,000 runs and 86 wickets in his 117 one-day internationals.

NETHERLANDS

Colours

Orange.

First one-day international

1996 v New Zealand at Vadodara (World Cup).

History

The Dutch have played cricket since the 19th century, but the game has only been played on a wider scale since the early 1980s. In the 20 years that followed, the Dutch recorded some famous victories against touring sides – West Indies and England included – and qualified for four World Cups. In 2003, they recorded their only win at this level, beating Namibia in the group stage.

Pocket Fact 🏏

The 1999 World Cup was held in England and Wales, and though the Netherlands hadn't qualified for the tournament, they were able to host one of the games — between Kenya and South Africa at Amstelveen.

SCOTLAND

Colours
Red and blue.

First one-day international
1999 v Australia at Worcester (World Cup).

History
Scotland can probably claim the oldest connections with cricket of any associate member — records show that the game was being played way back in the mid-1780s. The team have continued to play games against touring sides ever since and participate in English Sunday league cricket as well as cup competitions. Scotland qualified for the 1999 and 2007 World Cups.

Pocket Fact 🏏

Despite being old enemies on the football and rugby ground, England and Scotland's first one-day international cricket game didn't happen until 2008. Unfortunately the game was washed out after Scotland's innings.

🏏 OTHER CRICKETING NATIONS 🏏

Despite the relatively small number of professional cricketing nations, the game has a global appeal. As well as the 16 full and associate one-day international members, the ICC has awarded associate membership to a further 35 countries and affiliate membership to 60 countries, meaning cricket is played in more than 100 countries around the world. Here are some of the leading amateur nations:

- **Argentina.** Cricket was first played in Argentina in 1868, with a game against Uruguay. Since then the game in South America, and in Argentina in particular, has had highs and lows, with the high point being victory over the MCC in 1912.

- **Bermuda.** The first game played by Bermuda was in 1891. After gaining ICC membership in 1966, cricket has steadily flourished in the country and the highlight for Bermudan cricket to date was participation in the 2007 World Cup.

- **Germany.** The game of cricket has come late to Germany, with the country's first game played in 1995, against Austria in the European Nations Cup. But thanks to a largely ex-pat team, Germany have steadily grown in stature and now compete in the World Cricket League.

- **Gibraltar.** One of the better teams in Europe, Gibraltar have a rich cricketing history as the game has been played on 'the rock' since the late 18th century. The team have twice won division two of the European Championships.

- **Japan.** Cricket started in Japan with the Yokohama Cricket Club, where cricket is still played today. The national team first played in 1996 against Brunei.

- **Jersey.** The island of Jersey began playing cricket in 1957, with a game against neighbours Guernsey. Since then, Jersey have grown to be a strong force in European cricket, competing in division one of the European Championships.

- **United Arab Emirates.** Cricket has become a big game in the UAE since the country developed an international-standard stadium at Sharjah. The UAE side qualified for the 1996 World Cup, winning one game against the Netherlands.

- **USA.** Although the US share the record for the earliest international game with neighbours Canada, the game has only really resurfaced in the US in recent years. The high point was participation in the 2004 Champions Trophy.

Pocket Fact

One of the most famous teams in cricket is one with no home, and an archaic Italian name. I Zingari (meaning 'the gypsies') was formed by a collection of former students of Harrow School in England in 1845, but the club have no fixed home ground, playing all of their games on tour. I Zingari games were reported in Wisden until 2005. An Australian team of the same name was formed in 1888. Both teams are still active, making them among the oldest sporting clubs in the world.

8

THE GREAT GAMES

I tend to think that cricket is the greatest thing that God ever created on earth – certainly better than sex, although sex isn't too bad either.
Harold Pinter

Nothing beats a great game of cricket, whether you're playing it, watching from the stands or sitting at home with a cushion clutched to your chest, desperately willing one more wicket or a dozen more runs for victory. The thrilling climax of a test match, the desperate run chase in a one-day international, the explosive talent on display in Twenty20 – there are so many different ways to appreciate the game. It could be that you're left open-mouthed by a spectacular catch, run-out, innings or spell of bowling, or just by the sheer elegance and poise of a great player. Over the next two chapters we'll focus on the game of cricket at its best (and occasionally its worst) as we explore first the great games and then the individuals who make the game great.

● INTERNATIONAL COMPETITIONS ●

As part of the globalisation of cricket the ICC has introduced a series of competitions to build up the participation of emerging countries like Kenya, Ireland and Afghanistan. ICC competitions and leagues exist at all levels of cricket. Here's an overview of some of the key contests on the world stage.

THE WORLD CUP

Who qualifies?
All the test-playing nations plus the top four affiliate/associate nations from the World Cup Qualifier competition.

History

A one-day international competition, the World Cup began in 1975 and featured six test-playing nations (Australia, England, India, New Zealand, Pakistan and West Indies) as well as Sri Lanka and East Africa. It is played approximately every four years, with the 2011 tournament in India, Sri Lanka and Bangladesh.

Results

- 1975: hosts England; winners West Indies
- 1979: hosts England; winners West Indies
- 1983: hosts England; winners India
- 1987: hosts India/Pakistan; winners Australia
- 1992: hosts Australia/New Zealand; winners Pakistan
- 1996: hosts India/Pakistan/Sri Lanka; winners Sri Lanka
- 1999: hosts England; winners Australia
- 2003: hosts South Africa; winners Australia
- 2007: hosts West Indies; winners Australia

Pocket Fact

Australia have won the World Cup competition four times.

THE CHAMPIONS TROPHY

Who qualifies?

The top eight full-member teams, based on their position in the one-day international table.

History

Launched in 1998, the Champions Trophy was initially designed to generate revenue which would then be used to support cricket in developing nations. The early tournaments were a success and helped to promote the game in the host nations' countries, but eventually the competition lost its way – not helped by the fact that it never settled on a successful format.

Results

- 1998: hosts Bangladesh; winners South Africa

- 2000: hosts Kenya; winners New Zealand

- 2002: hosts Sri Lanka; winners no result (shared between Sri Lanka and India due to rain)

- 2004: hosts England; winners West Indies

- 2006: hosts India; winners Australia

- 2009: hosts South Africa; winners Australia

Pocket Fact

The 2013 Champions Trophy, due to be staged in England and Wales, is likely to be dropped in preference to a new test match world championship.

THE WORLD TWENTY20 CUP

Who qualifies?

All 10 test-playing nations plus top two qualifiers from World Twenty20 Qualifying tournament.

History

The most recent innovation by the ICC is one of the most profitable. The Twenty20 phenomenon was already well established by the time of the first tournament but it still brought the game to a whole new set of fans with its razzmatazz and spectacle. The first tournament saw some incredible milestones – including West Indies batsman Chris Gayle scoring 117 from 57 balls, Yuvraj Singh pummelling six sixes in one over from England's Stuart Broad (and becoming the first batsman to do so in an international match) and Australian Brett Lee taking a hat-trick for Australia against Bangladesh. The age of instant cricket had arrived.

Results

- 2007: hosts South Africa; winners India

- 2009: hosts England; winners Pakistan

- 2010: hosts West Indies; winners England

Pocket Fact

The next two World Twenty20 Cups will be held in 2012 and 2014, in Sri Lanka and Bangladesh respectively.

OTHER TOURNAMENTS

ICC World Cup Qualifier (formerly ICC Trophy)

As the name suggests, this is the competition which decides on the final make-up of the World Cup, with the top five teams in this tournament gaining automatic promotion to the main competition. Zimbabwe have won the competition the most (prior to gaining full ICC member status) with three victories. The competition was first played in 1979.

ICC Intercontinental Cup

Another ICC associate member tournament, this began in 2004 and has been won three times by Ireland. In 2009 the tournament changed to a new, two-tier format.

ICC World Cricket League

This is a regional tournament of eight divisions in which more than 80 associate and affiliate members of the ICC compete on a largely amateur basis.

Pocket Fact

Tickets and further information on all ICC tournaments are available from the ICC website at www.icc-cricket.yahoo.net.

● THE THREE GREATEST ●
ONE-DAY MATCHES

- **1999 Cricket World Cup semi-final, Edgbaston, England. Australia (213 all out) beat South Africa (213 all out) on superior run rate.** This game is notable just for the fact that both teams scored exactly the same – and all 20 wickets were taken. But the added drama in this story is that both sides performed so magnificently they each deserved to win. The cruelty of defeat was compounded for the South Africans by the fact that they were squeezed out of the tournament by the narrowest possible margin – an inferior run rate from a previous round.

- **2006 one-day international series, Johannesburg. South Africa (438–9) beat Australia (434–4) by one wicket.** Seven years later and the same teams emulated their incredible heroics in the World Cup with an even better game of cricket. Australia hit an incredible total of 400-plus – the first time this had been achieved in international limited overs cricket – and looked to be cruising to a resounding victory. But South Africa stunned the visitors with an amazing record-breaking innings which saw them secure victory with one ball remaining. Australia's Ricky Ponting made 164 but the honours were taken by South Africa's Herschelle Gibbs, whose 175 stands as one of the greatest one-day innings of all time.

- **2006 one-day international series, Lahore. India (292–5) beat Pakistan (288–8) by five wickets.** This might look like a simple victory on the face of it, but India v Pakistan is never simple, and the Pakistani bowler Mohammad Asif was in the form of his life going into this game. Pakistan's total was not huge, but with Asif bowling aggressively, they were confident of success. India were quickly reduced to 12–2 and looked like they were going to collapse when Sachin Tendulkar scored 95 to turn the match around. He missed out on a century, but has always regarded this as one of his better innings.

● TEST MATCH CRICKET ●

Playwright and cricket fanatic Tom Stoppard once said: 'I don't think I can be expected to take seriously a game which takes less than three days to reach its conclusion'. His comments were aimed at baseball, but might have just as easily represented those die-hard purists who say that nothing beats test match cricket for sheer delight. In this section we take a look at some of the greatest clashes ever seen, and some incredible old rivalries.

ENGLAND AND AUSTRALIA

The games between the two original test match nations provoke interest around the world for their competitive spirit. For the last 130 years, contests between these nations have been known as 'The Ashes' – and there have certainly been some fireworks down the years. The games are played on a strict rotation – in England they are played every four years on an odd numbered years. In Australia they are played over the break between an even numbered and an odd numbered year, for example 2014–2015. Venues for the Ashes tests are decided by the individual cricket boards but certain tests have become fixtures of the Ashes calendar – Lord's and Melbourne and always eagerly anticipated venues.

The origin of the Ashes

The Ashes is the name given to all test match cricket played between England and Australia, and which is represented by a small urn kept on permanent display at Lord's (and the facsimiles which are given to the victorious teams). The name of the contest doesn't come from the urn, however, but from England's first defeat by Australia in England, way back in 1882, some five years after the birth of test cricket.

The defeat took place at the Oval cricket ground in August. The day after, a mock obituary was published in The Sporting Times *newspaper which read:*

In Affectionate Remembrance
of
ENGLISH CRICKET
which died at the Oval
on
29th August 1882
Deeply Lamented by a large circle of sorrowing
Friends and Acquaintances
RIP
NB The body will be cremated and the
ashes taken to Australia

The media dubbed England's next trip to Australia as a quest
'to regain the Ashes', and the name has stuck. On that trip,
England captain Ivo Bligh was given a gift of the small
terracotta urn that is now at Lord's. It is believed to be filled
with the ashes of cricket bails.

The greatest Ashes series

In 2005, the Australians came to England with three of the greatest players who had ever played test match cricket – Ricky Ponting, Glenn McGrath and Shane Warne. They had held the Ashes since 1989, convincingly winning eight successive series. England, by contrast, were a young side albeit with some talented players. Here's the story in brief:

- **The first test.** A comfortable victory for the Australians suggested the pattern of history was to continue.

- **The second test.** Australia lost McGrath to a freak injury in the warm-up before the game and England won by the narrowest of margins – just two runs.

- **The third test.** The game was affected by the rain and eventually drawn thanks to a superbly defensive display of batting from Ponting and an Australian team on the back foot.

- **The fourth test.** England made a huge first innings total, bowled Australia out cheaply and made them follow-on – an almost unheard-of situation for the Aussies. Australia's second innings was much better and they set England a challenging total which they reached incredibly nervously with three wickets to spare.

- **The fifth test.** Australia were much more confident and England more defensive, but thanks to an outstanding century from Kevin Pietersen, the home team held out for a draw and won the series 2–1.

The overviews above can't convey the cut and thrust and intrigue of a test series between two evenly matched sides, but great observers of the game – like the legendary Australian commentator Richie Benaud – described it as the finest in living memory.

The latest Ashes series

The 2010–2011 series in Australia was billed as a turning point for both teams. For Australia it was a chance to regain the Ashes and to re-establish themselves after a dismal year which had seen them slump to fourth in the world rankings. For England the goal was even more significant, they needed to retain the Ashes on Australian soil – something they hadn't done for 24 years.

The first test match of the series at Brisbane suggested that it was to be a fairly even contest. Although England made an extraordinary 517-1 declared in their second innings, the game was eventually drawn and honours were even. The second test at Adelaide saw another massive England total – a first innings of 620-5 declared – which helped them to crush the Australians by an innings.

The third test at Perth saw the pendulum swing wildly back to the Australians' favour as England were dismissed cheaply twice and lost by a huge margin. The teams went into the fourth test with the series finely balanced, but from the first day – when Australia were skittled out for just 98 – England held the upper hand and won the game with ease by another huge innings margin.

In the final test at Sydney, England secured a record-breaking third innings victory away from home in a series to take the Ashes 3 matches to 1. England had achieved their objective of retaining the Ashes and Australia were left wondering what they could do to rebuild after a disastrous year.

Pocket Fact

They may have crumbled to defeat, but Australia went into the 2010–2011 Ashes series with typical confidence. The team had a giant image beamed onto the Palace of Westminster in London in October 2010, bearing a slogan which read 'Don't forget to pack the urn'. Unfortunately, the local council was not impressed and threatened legal action against the Aussies.

Ashes to Ashes: the best of the rest

- **1932–1933:** The notorious 'Bodyline' series in Australia saw a devastating tactic employed by the England bowlers. To counter the threat posed by great players like Don Bradman, the English bowled short on leg stump with the specific aim of causing the ball to jump and strike the batsmen on the body. A number of batsmen were injured and much ill-feeling was created (see p. 142 for more details). But the tactic had one 'positive' result – England won the series 4–1.

- **1948:** The final tour led by Bradman saw England soundly beaten 4–0 at home. It was Bradman's last series and the overall dominance of his side earned them the title of 'The Invincibles'. They played a total of 31 games on the tour and didn't lose a single one.

- **1956:** England's Jim Laker dominated the series with his incredibly disciplined spin bowling. After taking six wickets in an innings to help defeat the Australians at Headingley, Laker went into overdrive at Old Trafford, producing match figures of 19–90, the best bowling figures ever seen in professional cricket. Rarely has one man controlled a series as much as Laker did in 1956. He finished with a total of 46 wickets.

- **1981:** A series of two halves in England, with rookie England captain Ian Botham the villain of the first two tests, one draw and one defeat for the home side being enough to cause his resignation. But Botham came to life in the third game and masterminded three straight wins in a series still known as 'Botham's Ashes'.

- **1993:** Young spin bowler Shane Warne tossed up his first ball in Ashes cricket to the experienced England batsman Mike Gatting. The ball pitched well outside the leg stump and Gatting was happy to let it pass harmlessly through to the wicketkeeper. Instead, it turned almost 90 degrees and clattered into his stumps. Dubbed 'the ball of the century', it was the perfect calling card for the greatest bowler in Ashes history and a symbol of many years of Australian Ashes dominance.

Pocket Fact

Australian brewer and cricket sponsor Victoria Bitter (VB) offered to buy every adult in Australia a beer if their team won back the Ashes in the 2010–2011 series against England. The cost of the exercise would have been huge, with more than 13 million potential customers, but Australia lost the series 3-1 and VB kept the beer.

PAKISTAN AND INDIA

The intensity of the rivalry between India and Pakistan owes as much to politics as it does to sport and there have been long periods of inactivity when the teams have refused to play each other – or when it has been dangerous to do so for security reasons.

Having said that when the two do get together in the spirit of the game, the results are often extraordinary, and some of the finest test matches ever have been fought between these uneasy neighbours. Here are some of the best:

- **2004: Pakistan v India first test match, Multan. India won by an innings and 52 runs.** This game was notable for being India's first victory on Pakistani soil, but also for the incredible batting of Virender Sehwag and Sachin Tendulkar. Sehwag scored 309 and became the first Indian to hit 300-plus. Spinner Anil Kumble took 6–30 in the Pakistan second innings to wrap up the victory.

- **1999: India v Pakistan two-match series. First test, Chennai – Pakistan won by 12 runs.** This series was probably the greatest advertisement for Indian and Pakistani cricket. The first game was a close contest – chasing a victory target of 271 to win in the fourth innings, India were reduced to 82–5 and facing certain defeat. Yet again Sachin Tendulkar produced an incredible innings – of 136 runs – to bring his side into contention. They fell 12 runs short thanks to some brilliant bowling by Pakistan's Saqlain Mushtaq.

- **Second test, Delhi – India won by 212 runs.** The second test was even more extraordinary. A low-scoring contest was dominated by spin bowling. Saqlain was again dominant for Pakistan, along with his spinning partner Mushtaq Ahmed. But it was India's Anil Kumble who stole the headlines with a magnificent 14-wicket haul in the match – including all 10 Pakistani wickets in the fourth innings of the game. He was only the second bowler (after Jim Laker) to take a 10-wicket haul in an international innings. The series was a draw and cricket was the winner.

Central contracts – a poisoned chalice?

One of the most controversial improvements to the world of test match cricket over the last decade has been the introduction of central contracts for leading players in all test-playing nations. These contracts tie a specific group of players to international duty and crucially they limit those players' involvement in their domestic game. The exact number of contracts awarded varies from country to country, but in England they are awarded to 11 players. This can mean that a county's best players will play only a handful of domestic games in a season.

The advantage of central contracts is that it is easier to keep a group of players fit and available for test matches and other international games. They can also be very lucrative for the players, who can earn a reported £450,000 in fees. In England, where central contracts were introduced in 2000, the results have been very positive for the test team's success and consistency.

Not all players feel the benefit of central contracts, however, as they are often unable to play in tournaments such as the Indian Premier League because of their commitment to the contract. One high profile dissenter was former England all-rounder Andrew Flintoff, who famously rejected a central contract to give himself the flexibility to play where and when he wanted.

If tournaments such as the IPL continue to prosper it is possible that the central contract system will have to adapt to permit players to be involved, otherwise they may reject the contracts wholesale and make the whole idea redundant.

THE GREATEST TESTS

There are always rivalries between teams – though none as marked as those listed above. Neighbours will always want to beat neighbours, revenge will always be sought for past humiliations. That's why test cricket produces games like the following selection:

- **1958: West Indies v Pakistan at Bridgetown.** It might seem strange to start with a drawn match, but this was an example of cricket's ability to produce excitement even when there's no 'positive result'. An incredible first innings score of 579–9 declared (including Everton Weekes's 197) put the host side in a strong position – one which was underlined by Pakistan's collapse to 106 all out. The Pakistanis were forced to follow-on and batting second time around, their opening batsman Hanif Mohammad made an incredible 337 runs in part of a total of 657–8 declared. The game was drawn, and Hanif Mohammad was a hero, single-handedly saving a test match with his brilliance.

- **1960: Australia v West Indies at Brisbane.** The first test in a series of five began promisingly for the tourists when they hit 453 runs in their first innings, including a magnificent century from Gary Sobers. But Australia hit back with 505 and then bowled West Indies out for 284 in their second innings, leaving a challenging victory target of 233. Aussie all-rounder Alan Davidson, who took 10 wickets in the match, scored a valuable 80 to take his team to the edge of victory when disaster struck: four wickets fell for six runs and the game – the first in 80-plus years of test cricket – ended in a tie with the scores level.

- **1999: West Indies v Australia at Bridgetown.** The same foes, but a different result under extremely tense conditions. Australia started strongly with an imposing 490 in their first innings – Steve Waugh top-scoring with 199. West Indies replied with 329 and then surprised the Aussies in the second innings, bowling them out for just 146. Even so, a victory target of 308 was a tall order, made even more unlikely when the hosts slumped to 105–5. But an extraordinary innings by Brian Lara saw his team through to the narrowest of wins (by just one wicket). Lara finished unbeaten on 153.

- **2001: India v Australia at Eden Gardens, Kolkata.** Another strong Australian side made another impressive first innings total – their 445 owing much to captain Steve Waugh's 110. India were bowled out cheaply in their first innings for just 171 and were made to bat again by the Aussies. And how they batted – an incredible total of 657–7 declared, the cornerstone of which was VVS Laxman's 281. More excitement was to come in the final innings of the game when Australia slumped from 166–3 to 212 all out, thanks to six wickets from bowler Harbhajan Singh, whose seven wickets in the Australian first innings had included the first Indian hat-trick in tests. India won the game – and with it the most amazing turnaround in world cricket history – by 171 runs, the same total as their fateful first innings score.

● THE RECORD BREAKERS ●

As we've already discovered, cricket is a haven for lovers of all things statistical – from the Duckworth–Lewis method to the endless analysis of bowling/batting averages to determine the greatest players of all time, there's no other game that turns numbers into symbols of worship. So for all those who can't resist a decent stat – here's a selection of the finest:

PLAYER STATISTICS

Six of the best – the leading test match wicket-takers of all time

1. 800 Muttiah Muralitharan (Sri Lanka)

2. 708 Shane Warne (Australia)

3. 619 Anil Kumble (India)

4. 563 Glenn McGrath (Australia)

5. 519 Courtney Walsh (West Indies)

6. 434 Kapil Dev (India)

Six of the best – the best bowling figures in a test match innings

1. 10–53 Jim Laker for England v Australia, 1956

2. 10–74 Anil Kumble for India v Pakistan, 1999

3. 9–28 George Lohmann for England v South Africa, 1896

4. 9–37 Jim Laker for England v Australia, 1956

5. 9–51 Muttiah Muralitharan for Sri Lanka v Zimbabwe, 2002

6. 9–52 Richard Hadlee for New Zealand v Australia, 1985

Six of the best – the leading test match run-scorers of all time

1. 14,240* Sachin Tendulkar (India)

2. 12,250* Ricky Ponting (Australia)

3. 11,953 Brian Lara (West Indies)

4. 11,707* Rahul Dravid (India)

5. 11,174 Allan Border (Australia)

6. 11,126* Jacques Kallis (South Africa)

* to November 2010

Pocket Fact

Only eight batsmen have made more than 10,000 runs in test cricket. The first to reach the milestone was India's Sunil Gavaskar. No English batsman has yet made more than 10,000 runs – the highest scoring English player is Graham Gooch with 8,900.

Six of the best – the highest test match innings of all time

1. 400 (not out) Brian Lara for West Indies v England, 2004

2. 380 Matthew Hayden for Australia v Zimbabwe, 2003

3. 375 Brian Lara for West Indies v England, 1994

4. 374 Mahela Jayawardene for Sri Lanka v South Africa, 2006

5. 365 (not out) Gary Sobers for West Indies v Pakistan, 1958

6. 364 Len Hutton for England v Australia, 1938

Pocket Fact ✐

West Indian Brian Lara holds the record for highest test score and for the highest first-class score — 501 (not out) for Warwickshire against Durham in the English County Championship in 1994.

Six of the best – the leading test match catchers of all time

1. 198* Rahul Dravid (India)

2. 181 Mark Waugh (Australia)

3. 174* Ricky Ponting (Australia)

4. 171 Stephen Fleming (New Zealand)

5. 164 Brian Lara (West Indies)

6. 161* Mahela Jayawardene (Sri Lanka)

* to November 2010

Six of the best – the leading test match wicketkeepers of all time (dismissals – caught and stumped)

1. 504* Mark Boucher (South Africa)

2. 416 Adam Gilchrist (Australia)

3. 395 Ian Healy (Australia)

4. 355 Rod Marsh (Australia)

5. 270 Jeff Dujon (West Indies)

6. 269 Alan Knott (England)

* to November 2010

TEAM STATISTICS

Six of the best – the highest test match innings scores of all time

1. 952–6 declared by Sri Lanka v India, 1997

2. 903–7 declared by England v Australia, 1938

3. 849 by England v West Indies, 1930

4. 790–3 declared by West Indies v Pakistan, 1958

5. 765–6 declared by Pakistan v Sri Lanka, 2009

6. 760–7 declared by Sri Lanka v India, 2009

Six of the worst – the lowest test match innings scores of all time

1. 26 by New Zealand v England, 1955

2. 30 by South Africa v England, 1896

3. 30 by South Africa v England, 1924

4. 35 by South Africa v England, 1899

5. 36 by South Africa v Australia, 1932

6. 36 by Australia v England, 1902

Olympic cricket

Cricket enthusiasts have long argued for the game to be included in the Olympics – it was part of the Commonwealth Games in 1998 – but few realise that it was once an Olympic sport. In the 1900 Summer Games a team from Great Britain played a team from France (mainly composed of English ex-pats working in Paris) – but they were the only two competitors. Great Britain won the game, and the gold medal. Cricket has never been included as an Olympic discipline since then because the Olympic authorities argue that there are too few nations in the world that play the game to a professional standard and as such it is a 'minority' sport – try telling that to a billion fans in India and Pakistan. The advent of Twenty20 may at least provide a glimmer of hope for the future as it is a format that would fit easily into an Olympic schedule.

9

THE GREAT PLAYERS

It is as well for us to remember when we are watching the best batsmen that, however easy it may all look, they do not achieve their success without toil and sweat.
EW Swanton

How do you define a great player? One noted for his lifetime achievements perhaps? Or for flashes of individual brilliance? Or maybe even for the inspiration and guidance he has given to others? The answer is all of the above and plenty more besides. In this chapter we focus on what makes a player great – and what the all-time greats have achieved in their careers to guarantee their legendary status. We also take a look at the careers of some of the more notorious figures in world cricket.

⬤ THE LEGENDS OF THE GAME ⬤

Choosing an all-time world XI is a huge task and one that is almost entirely subjective. While some players' records speak for themselves – such as the ubiquitous Donald Bradman, an ever-present on each and every legends XI – others compete with half a dozen rivals for each place in the team.

The team listed below is intended to give as broad a geographical spread as possible – but it's also a tantalisingly exciting line-up.

THE BEST OF THE BEST – A WORLD XI

1. Jack Hobbs

2. Barry Richards

3. Donald Bradman (captain)

4. Sachin Tendulkar

5. Vivian Richards

6. Garfield Sobers

7. Wasim Akram

8. Alan Knott (wicketkeeper)

9. Richard Hadlee

10. Shane Warne

11. Muttiah Muralitharan

OPENING BATSMAN: JACK HOBBS (1882–1963)

Right-handed batsman

Team

England.

Record

Test matches: 51 tests; 5410 runs; 56.94 batting average.

First-class career: 61,237 runs; 50.65 batting average.

Claim to fame

Jack Hobbs was regarded as a complete batsman. His nickname was 'the master' and he lived up to it – bridging the gap from the final days of WG Grace and the early days of test match cricket to the golden age of Bradman. Hobbs had incredible longevity, playing for England until the age of 47 and for his county team until well into his fifties. His opening partnerships with Herbert Sutcliffe were the stuff of legend for the English national team in the 1920s.

Pocket Fact

Jack Hobbs's most notable feat was the number of centuries he scored in his career – 197 (including 15 for England). He had a habit of getting himself out soon after he'd reached the hundred mark – just to let someone else have a try!

The second XI choice: Len Hutton (1916–1990)

Another great English opener, Hutton once held the world record for the highest score in test match cricket – 364 against Australia in 1938 – made when he was only 22 years old.

OPENING BATSMAN: BARRY RICHARDS (1945–)

Right-handed batsman

Team

South Africa.

Record

Test matches: 4 tests; 508 runs; 72.57 batting average.

First-class career: 28,358 runs; 54.74 batting average.

Claim to fame

It may seem a little odd to include a man who played just four test matches in the world greats XI, but Barry Richards's talent was obvious even from the briefest international career. His chance to shine on the world stage was curtailed by South Africa's absence from the test arena following their ban in 1970, but his extraordinary career batting average shows him to be a batsman of exceptional ability. Despite being restricted to domestic cricket in South Africa and England as well as a starring role in Packer's World Series, Richards made a huge contribution to the game.

Pocket Fact

Richards was also an extremely useful off-break bowler. In his career, he took 77 wickets and had a best bowling return of 7 for 63.

The second XI choice: Matthew Hayden (1971–)

A great Australian test cricketer, Hayden averaged over 50 and also briefly held the world record for the highest score in test matches – a magnificent 380 against Zimbabwe.

NUMBER THREE (AND CAPTAIN): DONALD BRADMAN (1908–2001)

Right-handed batsman

Team

Australia.

Record

Test matches: 52 tests; 6,996 runs; 99.94 batting average.

First-class career: 28,067 runs; 95.14 batting average.

Claim to fame

'The Don', as he was affectionately known, was truly the godfather of cricket, a player so huge in stature that his equal will almost certainly never be seen. His rise to superstardom was swift and he was just 22 years old when he toured England for the first time, scoring 974 runs in the test series, including a then world record total of 334 at Headingley (309 of which was scored in just one day's play). His dominance of bowling attacks led directly to England's infamous 'bodyline' bowling tactics in 1932–1933 (see p. 142). His final test series, again played against the old enemy England, was in 1948, when Bradman was 40 years old. Despite falling for 0 in his last innings, he led his side to a series victory.

Pocket Fact

Bradman had the most incredible 'eye' for the ball – he could judge his shots perfectly and often played in an unorthodox style. His perfect timing was attributed to the habit he had as a schoolboy of perfecting his batting technique with a cricket stump and a golf ball bounced against a wall.

The second XI choice: Brian Lara (1969–)

It's impossible not to include a cricketer whose contribution to the game far exceeds his contribution to the record books (see p. 125). Lara wasn't always a total team player, but he had the ability to turn a game around using his own power and ability.

NUMBER FOUR: SACHIN TENDULKAR (1973–)

Right-handed batsman

Team

India.

Record

Test matches (2010 figures): 177 tests; 14,692 runs; 56.94 batting average.

First-class career: 56,900 runs (approx.).

Claim to fame

Tendulkar – also known as 'the little master' – is the closest thing to a legend still playing the game of cricket, although as he was 37 years old at the time of writing, even his career may be drawing to a close. His most remarkable feat is his longevity. He made his test debut at 16 and scored his first century at 17. He has made almost all the records of cricket his own – the most test and one-day international runs scored, the most hundreds in test and one-day cricket, the only player to score 200 in a one-day international – the list goes on. His critics argue that he has made his runs in an era of largely average bowling attacks, but history will prove his greatness as a player.

Pocket Fact ⟋

While watching Tendulkar bat on TV in 1996, Don Bradman called his wife into the room and asked: 'Who does he remind you of?' The answer was clear – though Bradman had never seen himself bat the similarity was clear for all to see and the two great men became good friends.

The second XI choice: Sunil Gavaskar (1949–)

A brave and tenacious Indian stalwart, 'Sunny' was celebrated for his leadership style and his battling approach. He scored over 10,000 runs in tests and was equally comfortable playing games of attack or defence.

NUMBER FIVE: VIVIAN (VIV) RICHARDS (1952–)

Right-handed batsman

Team

West Indies.

Record

Test matches: 121 tests; 8,540 runs; 50.23 batting average.

First-class career: 36,212 runs; 49.4 batting average.

Claim to fame

Viv Richards was one of the most stylish and powerful cricketers of any age. His ability to destroy bowling attacks as part of the fearsome West Indies side of the 1970s and 1980s was legendary. A fearless player of fast bowling, Richards never wore a helmet, but played forward to the bowling and was never better than when driving the ball straight down the ground for a mighty six.

Pocket Fact

Viv Richards still holds the record for the fastest ever test match century – scored in Antigua in 1986 against England. He reached 103 from just 56 balls (the second 50 coming from 21). England bowler John Emburey said it was 'The biggest carnage I have ever seen in such a short space of time in any first-class game.'

The second XI choice: Javed Miandad (1957–)

One of the greatest Pakistani batsmen, Miandad was also a tenacious player who was as much at ease in the short form of the game as in test matches. He was another whose test match average exceeded 50.

BATTING ALL-ROUNDER: GARFIELD (GARY) SOBERS (1936–)

Team

West Indies.

Record

Test matches: 93 tests; 235 wickets; 8,032 runs.

First-class career: 1,043 wickets; 28,315 runs.

Claim to fame

Gary Sobers is an incredibly strong candidate for the title of best all-round cricketer of all time. His batting was superbly powerful and effective. For many years he held the record for the highest score in test match cricket – 365 (not out). But he was also an incredibly useful bowler with a remarkable ability to switch from a fast pace early on in an innings to a slow pace when required later on. He was an inspirational captain for the West Indies and also captained the Rest of the World sides which played England and Australia in 1970–1971 instead of the banned South Africans. In true style, his contribution to the first of these games was to take 6 for 21 in England's first innings then follow up with a score of 183.

Pocket Fact

For all his all-round brilliance in the test match arena, Sobers will probably be best remembered for something he did in English county cricket – being the first man to perform the remarkable feat of scoring six sixes in an over. Sobers hit 36 in six balls off Glamorgan bowler Malcolm Nash in 1968.

The second XI choice: Kapil Dev (1959–)

A great batsman and fast bowler, but an even greater captain who led by example and who helped India gain world recognition as a major force in the 1980s. He played a massive 131 test matches in his illustrious career.

BOWLING ALL-ROUNDER: WASIM AKRAM (1966–)

Team

Pakistan.

Record

Test matches: 104 tests; 414 wickets; 2,898 runs.

First-class career: 1,042 wickets; 7161 runs.

Claim to fame

Though not the most gifted batsman, Wasim Akram was a truly great left-arm bowler – possibly the best there's ever been. He turned the skill of swing bowling (getting the ball to move late through the air) into an incredible art form, and took many wickets with deliveries that seemed to swerve first one way and then the other through the air. Though he's often in the shadow of similarly great players like Imran Khan and Waqar Younis it is Akram's sheer vitality and hunger for the game that marks him out as a true legend.

Pocket Fact

Despite having a poor batting average, Akram will always be remembered for one extraordinary innings – a massive 257 (not out) which he scored against Zimbabwe in 1996–1997.

Second XI choice: Ian Botham (1955–)

'Beefy' Botham doesn't have the finest statistics in world cricket, but he is one of the finest competitors the game ever produced. He scored more than 5,000 test runs and took nearly 400 wickets.

WICKETKEEPER: ALAN KNOTT (1946–)

Team

England.

Record

Test matches: 95 tests; 4,389 runs; 250 catches.

First-class career: 18,105 runs; 1,211 catches.

Claim to fame

Every great team needs a great wicketkeeper and Alan Knott was one of the finest – an athlete, a brave and skilled batsman and an inspirational figure on the field, Knott was famous for keeping himself in superb physical condition. Many greats have followed Knott – Ian Healy, Adam Gilchrist (see below) and Mark Boucher included – but no-one has matched the tenacity and sheer exuberance of England's best ever wicketkeeper.

Pocket Fact

Knott's obsession with his physical condition was so extraordinary that he would use any small break in play as an opportunity to start his limbering-up exercises all over again.

The second XI choice: Adam Gilchrist (1971–)

With more than 800 first-class dismissals and 5,570 test runs at an average close to 50, Gilchrist is a truly great all-round cricketer. Not in the same athletic league as Knott, he is nonetheless a brilliant batsman with several match-saving innings to his name.

BOWLER: RICHARD HADLEE (1951–)

Team

New Zealand.

Record

Test matches: 86 tests; 431 wickets; 3,124 runs.

Career: 1,490 wickets; 12,052 runs.

Claim to fame

Hadlee is the finest cricketer ever to come out of New Zealand and one of the most feared and effective fast bowlers of any time. More than anyone, he was responsible for the rising influence of New Zealand in the 1980s, and his wickets helped secure series wins over England and crucial victories over the old enemy Australia. He was the first bowler ever to break through the 400 wicket barrier and was a steady and calm batsman, always ready to dig in and fight for his country.

Pocket Fact ✎

To date, Richard Hadlee is the only cricketer ever to receive a knighthood while still playing the game professionally.

The second XI choice: Imran Khan (1952–)

The last of the great 1980s all-rounders (following Hadlee, Botham and Kapil Dev) and probably the most charismatic of the bunch. He was a great leader on the pitch, famously brave and competitive, and his record in just 88 test matches is among the best around.

BOWLER: SHANE WARNE (1969–)

Team

Australia.

Record

Test matches: 145 tests; 708 wickets; 25.41 bowling average (runs per wicket). Career: 1,319 wickets.

Claim to fame

In any other time, Shane Warne would be the finest cricketer of his generation, but as he shared the stage with Tendulkar and Muralitharan it's pretty tough to choose between them as modern greats. He broke into test cricket with a bang, bemusing England in the Ashes test series of 1993 (see p. 120) and continued to save his best bowling for Ashes encounters. Warne probably edges Muralitharan out for sheer range of ability and tenacity, but he will always be best known as a pivotal part of the almost unbeatable Australian side of the decade from 1995–2005.

Pocket Fact ✎

Shane Warne was a very useful batsman too — scoring a total of 3,154 runs in tests, but he never made a century. Maddeningly, his top score in tests was 99.

The second XI choice: Glenn McGrath (1970–)

It seems only fitting that the replacement for Warne in a second-string team would be the player he frequently worked in tandem with in test cricket – and to such devastating effect. McGrath's 563 test wickets make him the most successful fast bowler in the world.

BOWLER: MUTTIAH MURALITHARAN (1972–)

Team

Sri Lanka.

Record

Test matches: 133 tests; 800 wickets; 22.72 bowling average (runs per wicket). Career: 1,374 wickets.

Claim to fame

'Murali', as he is known, is a true enigma. His unorthodox bowling style has seen him labelled as 'genius', 'enigma' or 'cheat' by different commentators. The last and most serious of these allegations threatened to blight his career when his bowling action was repeatedly challenged by umpires in the 1990s. But after a series of investigations, his action – and his amazing ability to sharply spin the ball – were shown to be legitimate and he rightly takes his place among the true greats of world cricket. His world record test wicket total will almost certainly be beaten one day by another genius, but few players will match his humility and generosity – Murali was one of the cricketers who gave their time and money to help after the Asian tsunami destroyed large areas of the Sri Lankan coastline.

Pocket Fact

Muttiah Muralitharan reached his extraordinary 800 wicket landmark in the most incredible circumstances – it came with the final ball in his final test match as he had the Indian number 11 batsman caught behind to win the match.

The second XI choice: Anil Kumble (1970–)
A quieter man in the shadows of Warne and Murali, India's Kumble was nonetheless gifted and produced 619 test wickets in a career spanning 132 test matches. His incredible 16-wicket match return against Pakistan (see p. 121) is the most memorable of his many match-winning feats.

Pocket Fact

In 2010, leading cricket website cricinfo.com produced an all-time greatest XI, selected by a panel of cricket experts from all over the world. Their choice was as follows: Jack Hobbs, Len Hutton, Don Bradman, Sachin Tendulkar, Viv Richards, Gary Sobers, Adam Gilchrist, Malcolm Marshall, Shane Warne, Wasim Akram, Dennis Lillee.

Knights of the cricket field

The following players have not only been awarded legendary status and respect, they have also been awarded a knighthood:

- *Sir Donald Bradman*
- *Sir Richard Hadlee*
- *Sir Garfield (Gary) Sobers*
- *Sir Vivian (Viv) Richards*
- *Sir Jack Hobbs*
- *Sir Len Hutton*
- *Sir Ian Botham*

● MORE THAN JUST CRICKETERS ●

Being an international cricketer would be enough of an achievement for most of us, but there is a select band of individuals who have gone on to make their names in other fields as well – different sports, politics, religion and even on film. Here are some of the most notable cross-over stars:

- **Kapil Dev.** As an icon of Indian cricket it's perhaps not surprising that Kapil Dev also made a name for himself pursuing India's other great passion, film. He is credited in four Bollywood feature films, in an acting career that spans 25 years.

- **Ian Botham.** In his heyday of the late 1970s and early 1980s, England cricketer Ian Botham also played football for Scunthorpe United.

- **Denis Compton.** The original 'Brylcreem' boy – Denis Compton was more than just an endorser of hair products, he was one of the game's first superstars. He played for England's cricket team more than 70 times and also represented Arsenal FC and England at international football.

- **Imran Khan.** Pakistani all-rounder Imran Khan retired from cricket in 1992. Since then he has devoted his efforts to two areas – social work and politics. He has become one of Pakistan's leading opposition politicians, and while he has never tasted real power, his status as a cricket legend gives him a higher-than-usual profile outside his country.

- **Viv Richards.** Richards is a rarity as he is one of the few sportsmen to represent his country in world cups in two different games. He played in many Cricket World Cups for West Indies and also played football for Antigua in a World Cup qualifying game.

- **David Sheppard.** Another England cricketer, Sheppard played 22 tests for his country, before retraining as a priest and eventually rising through the Anglican church to become Bishop of Liverpool.

- **Ken Hough.** A cricketer and footballer, Hough represented New Zealand in both his skills areas, and also managed to play football for Australia.

- **Craig Evans.** Evans is a cricketer and rugby union player who has represented Zimbabwe in both games.

- **Biddy Anderson.** South African Anderson played test cricket and rugby union for his country from 1894–1902.

Pocket Fact ✐

The players listed above are impressive examples of multi-skilled individuals, but no-one beats Charles Burgess (CB) Fry, who represented England at cricket and football in the early part of the 20th century, played in an FA Cup final, equalled the world long jump record and reputedly turned down an offer to become King of Albania.

● THE BAD BOYS OF CRICKET ●

Even a game as noble as cricket must have its fair share of bad boys – though thankfully in the game's 400-plus year history there has only been a handful of truly shocking incidents and scandals. Here are some of the more notable examples of when scandal has stopped play.

The match fixers

As betting plays such an important part in cricket these days, it isn't surprising that the main scandals relating to the game involve fixing games for financial gain. From the 2010 spot-fixing allegations against members of the Pakistan cricket team to life bans for players like South African captain Hansie Cronje, Kenya's Maurice Odumbe and Indian batting legend Mohammad Azharuddin, greed and self-interest are unfortunate facets of the game, even at the highest level.

A body blow

The Ashes series in Australia in 1932–1933 will go down as one of the most hostile and shameful in history. The main source of the hostility was the so-called 'Bodyline' bowling tactic employed by the English bowlers – bowling short on leg stump and placing a large number of fielders on the leg side to take catches off batsmen who were defending themselves against physical danger. The England captain Douglas Jardine was an outspoken critic of the Australians, and famously followed a delivery by bowler Harold Larwood that had hit an Aussie batsman in the chest with the line

'Well bowled Harold'. A riot nearly ensued and Jardine remained a hate figure in Australia for years. The series led to some major changes in the laws, most notably restrictions on the leg side field.

TV interference

Australian media mogul Kerry Packer was attempting to negotiate TV rights with the ICC in 1976 when the discussions broke down and Packer vowed to set up his own rival world cricket competition. The World Series was born, although it was dubbed Packer's 'circus' by the media. Packer secured the services of England captain Tony Greig to play in the series and to help with promotion. Over two seasons – 1977 to 1978 – the World Series recruited many of the top stars from Australia, West Indies and England. Some nations prevented their stars from joining, some threatened bans for anyone who played. The game threatened to tear itself in two. But in 1979, Packer got the exclusive broadcasting deal he wanted and the status quo returned.

Rebels rebel

South Africa's exclusion from world cricket began in 1970 but by the beginning of the 1980s, the South African cricket authorities, led by Dr Ali Bacher, were keen to encourage touring sides. A group of English test players was encouraged to play a series of games in a move that shocked the cricket world and caused outrage in society as it was felt it legitimised the apartheid regime. All the players – and the Australians and West Indians who took part in subsequent tours until the nation's exclusion was lifted in 1991 – were given international bans ranging from three years to life.

Pocket Fact

The financier and philanthropist Allen Stanford, who was charged with fraud by American authorities in 2009, had been the host and main benefactor of a competition which boasted the largest prize in cricket history. The Stanford Superstars (a West Indies XI) played England in Antigua in 2008 for a prize of $20 million.

Zimbabwe's woes

Mark Vermeulen has been one of Zimbabwe cricket's leading performers since his debut in 2002. In 2004 he was struck on the head by a ball, an accident that changed his life forever. Two years later he was charged with setting fire to the Harare Sports Club and National Academy, though he was cleared at his trial when it emerged that the injury he'd suffered had caused epilepsy and other psychiatric problems. Despite this, he made an incredible comeback, returning to the Zimbabwe side in 2009.

Umpires strike back

Umpires are not known for being the centre of attention on the cricket field, but two names stand out as controversial figures. The first is Shakoor Rana, who had a very public and damaging row with England captain Mike Gatting in Faisalabad, Pakistan, when he accused Gatting of moving fielders as the bowler was running up to bowl (which is not allowed by the laws of the game). The two men traded insults and a day's play was lost in the test match as the incident escalated. Both men lost their jobs the following year.

Umpires strike back part II

The second scandal-hit umpire was Australian Darryl Hair who was involved in a number of incidents, most notably the fourth test match between England and Pakistan in 2006, when he and his fellow umpire Billy Doctrove accused Pakistan of tampering with the ball and awarded five penalty runs to England. The Pakistanis were so angered they refused to come back out after the tea interval and so Hair and Doctrove declared the test match forfeit and awarded England the win. Pakistan and England both subsequently agreed to play on but the umpires stuck to their guns. The scandal would have ended there, but it was later revealed that Hair had offered his resignation to the ICC in return for a one-off payment of US$500,000. Hair was later banned for 18 months by the ICC and eventually resigned from umpiring in 2008.

● SIX OF THE BEST 'MEN ● IN THE MIDDLE'

Unlike the unfortunate cases above, most of the men in the white coats who officiate at cricket matches at all levels in all parts of the world are fine and well-respected individuals. Here's a selection of some of the greatest men who have ever stood in the middle.

- **Harold 'Dickie' Bird.** One of the great umpires of the modern age, Dickie Bird was known for his down-to-earth Northern English humour and professional integrity. He umpired a total of 66 test matches from 1973–1996. In his final test as umpire – a game between England and India – the players formed a guard of honour to welcome him onto the field.

- **David Shepherd.** 'Shep' was probably the best-loved umpire in the world. An Englishman through and through, he umpired for 20 years at the highest level – his first test was in 1985, the last in June 2005 – and over this time he officiated in 92 tests. As well as being a brilliantly fair-minded umpire, he was known for his quirks. Famously superstitious, he would skip every time the score was on 111 (the dreaded 'Nelson' – see Chapter 7 and glossary) or multiples thereof.

- **Steve Bucknor.** When he retired in 2009, Jamaica-born Bucknor had umpired 128 tests in a 20-year career that saw a few lows but many highs. Like Dickie Bird, he received a guard of honour in his final game and a standing ovation from the crowd. While Bucknor was involved in a few controversies – the most high profile being the questionable final of the 2007 World Cup in which the game was finished in almost total darkness – he was well respected and extremely accurate. His nickname 'Slow Death' came from the incredibly slow and deliberate way he raised his finger to show a batsman was out.

- **Billy Bowden.** Like many umpires New Zealander Bowden began his life in cricket as a player. That's where his similarity to other umpires ends, however, as in his test match umpiring career to date he's established a niche as the most quirky, eccentric performer around. He has made each of the 'standard' umpiring signals his own with strange variations including his famous crooked finger raised to declare a batsman out – the finger is crooked because of the arthritis that plagued Bowden's playing career.

- **Rudi Koertzen.** South African Koertzen was the second umpire (after Bucknor) to reach 100 tests. He umpired 108 in an 18-year test career from 1992–2010. He's the first umpire in the history of the game to umpire in 100 tests and 200 one-day internationals. A very high-profile and well-respected umpire, Koertzen appears to have achieved the rare status of being an official who is liked and respected by all.

- **Daryl Harper.** As technology becomes a bigger part of the game, so the pressure on the umpires increases. This was certainly the case for Australian Daryl Harper, who found himself at the centre of a number of controversies relating to his role as third umpire (using TV monitors to act as a referral system) in international games. On one occasion – during a test between South Africa and England – Harper was asked to check whether batsman Graeme Smith had made contact with a ball, but did not turn up the volume on his monitor, and so consequently heard no noise, ruling the batsman not out. In spite of this and similar hiccups, Harper remains one of the game's leading and most respected officials.

The legacy of 'The Bearded Wonder'

Bill Frindall, was an enigma – a professional cricket scorer from 1966 until his death in 2009, he turned the sometimes maligned art of scoring into an art form, creating reams of statistical analysis which gained him a reputation as a living encyclopaedia of cricket. The nickname 'Bearded Wonder' was given by Brian Johnston, his colleague on the long-running BBC radio Test Match Special *– of which Frindall was the longest-serving presenter. Frindall also edited more than 20 editions of the* Playfair Cricket Annual *and many Wisden books of cricket statistics.*

THE CULTURE OF CRICKET

We welcome BBC World Service listeners to the Oval, where the bowler's Holding, the batsman's Willey.
Brian Johnston, BBC Test Match Special, 1976

The influence of cricket around the world is felt in more areas than just the sporting arena. Cricket is a massive business – from BBC radio to the Indian Premier League's live streaming on YouTube – but the game's relationship with other media hasn't always been successful. In this chapter, we take a look at cricket's relationship with popular culture and the ways in which it is depicted in film, fiction, on stage and on television.

● CRICKET COVERAGE ●

RADIO

There was a time when radio coverage was the only regular form of cricket commentary. BBC Radio 4's *Test Match Special* (TMS) dates back more than 50 years and its coverage of international cricket tournaments like the Twenty20 World Cup is rightly praised as the finest and most comprehensive in the world. TMS also has the admirable quality of impartiality – although the broadcast covers England cricket matches throughout the year, commentators and summarisers are brought in from the guest nations to add a touch of balance to proceedings.

The success of TMS in England has inspired other broadcasters – ABC in Australia, SABC in South Africa to name but two – to provide comprehensive radio and web broadcast services.

Six of the best – commentators

- John Arlott (England)
- Tony Cozier (West Indies)
- Richie Benaud (Australia)
- Rameez Raja (Pakistan)
- Sunil Gavaskar (India)
- Karunaratne Abeysekera (Sri Lanka)

Pocket Fact

Zimbabwean cricket commentator Dean Du Plessis is regarded as one of the finest commentators in the game – despite being totally blind. Du Plessis, who started commentating in 2001, uses his acute sense of hearing to interpret what's happening on the pitch – he can even recognise individual bowlers from their footfalls.

TELEVISION

Cricket has an uneasy relationship with television in some parts of the world – partially linked to the furore over Kerry Packer's breakaway league (see p. 143). In England, the rights to broadcast home test match cricket were traditionally owned by the BBC and were regarded as so-called 'crown jewels' rights – that is, ones which should never be sold. But they were sold – firstly to Channel 4 television and then to satellite broadcaster Sky, which already held the rights to televise overseas test matches.

One of the main criticisms aimed at television's involvement in cricket is that the start and end times of the day's play are now just as likely to be determined by the television producer as by the two teams – many observers fear that TV's demand for more excitement in the game is driving traditional elements, like the five-day test match, out of fashion.

However, throughout the world, cricket broadcasting rights are still big business – major broadcast networks like the Nine

Network in Australia and ESPN Star Sports in Pakistan pay a fortune to secure the exclusive rights in their area. Advertising revenue is the main driving force, but the huge fees paid by the networks also help to develop cricket at the grass roots level.

ONLINE

While television threatened the dominance of radio commentary, the advent of the internet has strengthened it – with radio commentary now available worldwide with incredible clarity. But the internet has allowed cricket to flourish in other ways. In 2010 the video sharing website YouTube signed a deal with the Indian Premier League to offer live streaming of all matches worldwide. This was the largest internet-based cricket broadcasting project to date and may be a sign that cricket is moving away from the traditional armchair market.

Cricket's online influence is also felt through the volume of information-sharing websites. For a game obsessed with facts, details and statistics, the sheer size and density of the web is the perfect partner.

Cricket online – a web XI

1. www.cricinfo.com – the ultimate statistics website.
2. www.indiancricketfans.com – a great overview of the game from an Indian perspective.
3. www.cricket365.com – another brilliant archive site in the style of cricinfo.
4. www.cricketwatch.org – an alternative take on the world of cricket.
5. www.pakpassion.net – a comprehensive site devoted to Pakistan cricket.
6. www.cricketweb.net – a very detailed cricket blog.
7. www.bbc.co.uk/cricket – the BBC's comprehensive cricket homepage includes country profiles and background to the game.
8. www.banglacricket.com – everything you need to know about cricket in Bangladesh.

9. *www.baggygreen.com.au – the most comprehensive Australian website.*

10. *www.blackcaps.co.nz – New Zealand's official site – great video clips archive.*

11. *www.caribbeancricket.com – an alternative take on the world of West Indian cricket.*

Cricket's famous fans – an all-time XI

1. The Dalai Lama, spiritual leader

2. Mick Jagger, musician

3. Eric Clapton, musician

4. Usain Bolt, 100 metres sprint world record holder

5. Sam Mendes, film and theatre director

6. JM Barrie, author and playwright

7. Michael Parkinson, British TV presenter

8. Russell Crowe, actor

9. Boris Karloff, horror movie star

10. Sir John Paul Getty, billionaire

11. Sir John Major, former British Prime Minister

● CRICKET ON THE PAGE ●

Nothing does cricket justice so much as the incredible volume of words devoted to it on the printed page. Non-fiction books devoted to the technique, history and characters of the game are many and varied. Biographies and autobiographies come out every year, some good, some inferior ghost-written cash-in efforts. But the true legends of cricket writing shine through the decades and they will always be the benchmark for all who follow.

- **Neville Cardus.** (1888–1975) Cardus was a writer with two great passions – cricket and music – and he managed to bring the lyricism of the latter to the former. He worked for many years at the *Manchester Guardian* and introduced a form of poetic cricket writing that has been often imitated and never beaten. Great works include: *The Summer Game*, *Good Days*, *Full Score* and *Close of Play*.

- **Mike Brearley.** (1942–) A legend of the game, whose fame has spread since his imperious captaincy of England in the late 1970s and – most famously – his return to the captaincy following Ian Botham's resignation in the legendary 1981 Ashes test series. His book, *The Art of Captaincy*, is widely regarded as the definitive work on the subject of leadership, both on the cricket pitch and off.

- **Gideon Haigh.** (1965–) An expert on Australian cricket and a fascinating chronicler of the modern game. His book *The Cricket War* is one of the finest accounts of the Packer circus scandal in the late 1970s (see p. 143). His biographies are excellent, especially *Mystery Spinner*, the story of Jack Iverson.

- **John Arlott.** (1914–1991) A commentator with an unforgettable voice, as rich as fruit cake, Arlott was also a prolific and highly talented writer. His biographies of Fred Trueman and Jack Hobbs are superb, as is his *Vintage Summer*, an evocation of a bygone age of cricket.

- **EW Swanton.** (1907–2000) Like Arlott, Swanton was a commentator on the BBC's *Test Match Special*, and was similarly a highly gifted author. His great books include *Sort of a Cricket Person*, *Cricket from All Angles* and *Last Over – a Life in Cricket*.

- **CLR James.** (1901–1989) James was born in Trinidad and Tobago. He wrote many books on politics and sport, but will be forever remembered for the legendary *Beyond a Boundary*, an autobiographical work that managed to combine its author's passion for the game with his fervent political views. It is frequently cited as the best book ever written on the game of cricket.

- **David Frith.** (1937–) One of the founders of the periodical *Wisden Cricket Monthly*, Frith is also one of the most elegant authors on the game – with particular focus on the Ashes series of tests. His greatest book is *Bodyline Autopsy* – a brilliant analysis of the legendary 'bodyline' series of tests in 1932.

- **Ramachandra Guha.** (1958–) One of India's finest authors on social, political and cricket issues. His greatest work is *A Corner of a Foreign Field: an Indian History of an English Sport*.

- **Jack Fingleton.** (1908–1981) Although Fingleton is regarded as one of the finest writers on cricket ever to come out of Australia his reputation is clouded by his lifelong feud with Don Bradman. However, his writing is undeniably superb, as evidenced by great biographical works such as *The Immortal Victor Trumper*.

Pocket Fact

The annual Authors v Actors game at Lord's was a fixture of the social season at the beginning of the 20th century. One such game in 1907 featured a host of famous names, including Sir Arthur Conan Doyle (creator of Sherlock Holmes), AA Milne (author of Winnie the Pooh*) and PG Wodehouse (creator of* Jeeves and Wooster*).*

Humorous cricket books – an all-time XI

1. *Rain Men* by Marcus Berkmann

2. *Fatty Batter* by Michael Simkins

3. *Penguins Stopped Play* by Harry Thompson

4. *Balham to Bollywood* by Chris England

5. *You Must Like Cricket – memoirs of an Indian cricket fan* by Soumya Bhattacharya

6. *Memoirs of a Twelfth Man* by Antony Couch

7. *Herbert Farjeon's Cricket Bag* by Herbert Farjeon

8. *Tales from the Long Room* (et al) by Peter Tinniswood

9. *And God Created Cricket* by Simon Hughes

10. *Many a Slip* by Gideon Haigh

11. *Bedside Cricket* by Christopher Martin-Jenkins

Wisden – the bible of cricket

The *Wisden Cricketers' Almanack* was first published in 1864, by legendary former cricketer John Wisden (see p. 11 for more details on Wisden's playing feats). It has been published every year for almost 150 years, making it the oldest sports annual in the world. Wisden contains a mixture of obituaries, comment, records and awards, including the well-known Wisden Cricketers of the Year awards, which date back as far as 1889. As well as sections on the English domestic and international scene, there are sections on cricket throughout the world.

Pocket Fact

A copy of the first edition of Wisden will cost you around £20,000 to buy today. The first hardback edition of the book, introduced in 1896, will cost anything up to £30,000.

Wisden trivia – an all-time XI

1. The first edition of Wisden cost one shilling (five pence sterling) and was 112 pages long.

2. The cover of Wisden didn't take on its distinctive yellow hue until 1938.

3. The famous woodcut of Victorian cricketers appeared on the cover in the same year.

4. The first actual person to be shown on the cover was England's captain Michael Vaughan in 2003.

5. EW Swanton's copy of the 1939 almanack went with him to a Japanese prisoner of war camp – both survived, and the

book, much-thumbed and appreciated by all the camp's prisoners, is now in Lord's Cricket Museum.

6. The title 'the bible of cricket' is never used by the publishers themselves.

7. The book has had just 16 editors in 146 years of publication.

8. In 2000, Wisden asked 100 cricket experts to name their five players of the century – the winners were Don Bradman, Jack Hobbs, Viv Richards, Shane Warne and Gary Sobers.

9. In 2009, Claire Taylor was chosen as one of the Wisden cricketers of the year – the only woman to date who has won the accolade.

10. The almanack didn't cover the first test match in 1877.

11. Throughout its publishing history, Wisden has always remained independent of the cricketing authorities.

🏏 CRICKET IN EVERYDAY LANGUAGE 🏏

As the influence of cricket has spread throughout the world over the last 300 years, it's not surprising that some of the game's key phrases have crept into our everyday language too. Here are seven of the most common examples of cricket's impact on English.

- **It's just not cricket** – used generally to mean something is unfair or against the normal rules of behaviour.

- **Play a straight bat** – to behave in a decent and honourable fashion.

- **Bowled over** – completely overwhelmed, possibly in a very positive context, as in 'I was bowled over by her beauty and charm'.

- **Stumped** – confused and utterly bewildered.

- **On the back foot** – behaving in a defensive manner.

- **Caught out** – deceived or misled, as in 'the students were caught out by the trick question in the exam'.

- **Hit for six** – taken completely by surprise, as in 'The news has hit me for six, to be honest'.

● CRICKET ON FILM ●

There's not much to be said for cricket's cinematic record, mainly because it has been largely ignored by Hollywood. However, the world's biggest film industry, Bollywood, in India, has produced some notable cricketing movies. Here are five typical examples from around the world:

- *Lagaan – once upon a time in India* **(2001).** Arguably the most successful rendition of cricket on screen, this Bollywood classic tells the story of a village cricket team playing the colonial masters in the days of the Raj. As a classic tale of David versus Goliath, it typifies the spirit of the game.

- *The Final Test* **(1953).** A British film, written by playwright Terence Rattigan and starring leading British TV actor Jack Warner as a cricketer who is desperate for his wayward son to watch his final innings. The drama is more emotional than cricketing, but it's an entertaining period piece.

- *Hansie* **(2008).** A drama documentary from South Africa chronicling the troubled and tragic life of the country's disgraced former captain Hansie Cronje.

- *Hit for Six* **(2009).** A Barbadian movie featuring a wealth of cameos from leading West Indies cricketers. Apparently created as an homage to *Lagaan*, but bearing closer comparison to *The Final Test*, this is the tale of a cricketer who overcomes allegations in order to impress his estranged father.

- *Out of the Ashes* **(2009).** A UK/Afghan documentary charting the remarkable rise of the Afghan cricket team from wartorn oblivion to international recognition.

Pocket Fact ✐

English comedian and cricket fan Rory Bremner released a pop song in 1985 called N-N-Nineteen Not Out, *a parody of an earlier hit,* 19 *by Paul Hardcastle. Bremner's comic song mocked the dismal performance of the England cricket team after the West Indies had thrashed them in the 1984 test match series. It reached number 13 in the UK charts.*

Six of the best cricket plays (or plays featuring cricket)

- *Outside Edge* by Richard Harris

- *The English Game* by Richard Bean

- *The No Boys Cricket Club* by Roy Williams

- *P'tang Yang Kipperbang* (TV play) by Jack Rosenthal

- *The Pope's Wedding* by Edward Bond

- *The Wit and Wisden of Martin Truelove* (radio play) by Dan Sefton

Cricket and charity

Cricket is essentially a social game, which may explain why so many former players like to keep their hands in with charity appearances. There are many teams around the world dedicated to raising money for good causes, including the following two of the best-loved and longest running teams:

Bunbury CC. *Founded by record producer Sir David English, the Bunburies have raised more than £12 million for good causes in 23 years. During this time many of the world's greatest cricketers have played for the team – from Ian Botham to Gordon Greenidge to Glenn McGrath – as well as some of the leading celebrities from the world of sport and entertainment. One of the most remarkable achievements of the Bunbury charity is the English Schools Cricket Association,* which is credited with nurturing the talents of many future first class cricketers, including 60 young players who have gone on to play for England.

The Lord's Taverners. Established more than 60 years ago, the Lord's Taverners team has always focused on making cricket, recreational activities and other sports accessible to young disadvantaged people and those with disabilities. The charity was initially established by a group of actors, and has many celebrity patrons, most notably Prince Philip, Duke of Edinburgh, who is the charity's official '12th man'. The Lord's Taverners stage charity cricket matches and other fund-raising events throughout the year.

THE CRICKET GLOSSARY

There is a widely held and quite erroneous belief that cricket is just another game.
HRH The Duke of Edinburgh

Agricultural shot (slang)
A wild cross-batted hit by a batsman, closely resembling a farm worker tossing hay around on a field. (See also cow corner).

Analysis
The statistical record in the scorebook showing the number of overs bowled by a bowler in an innings, along with the number of maidens, runs conceded and wickets.

Anthea (slang)
A pitch that takes spin well, often because it is uneven or cracked, is sometimes referred to as a 'turner' ie it will help the ball to turn. The nickname is derived from the surname of British TV personality Anthea Turner.

Appeal
A shout from the bowler and/or fielding cricketers to get the umpire's opinion as to whether a batsman has been caught, lbw (leg before wicket) or stumped/run out. It takes the form of the famous question 'How's that?'

Arm ball
This is a kind of delivery from a spin bowler that doesn't actually spin, just coming straight – and fast – towards the batsman.

Ashes

The name given to the contest between England and Australia at test match level. The name derives from the notice published in an English newspaper following England's first home defeat by Australia in 1882, telling of the death of English cricket and stating that the 'ashes' would be taken to Australia. A small terra-cotta urn, presented to England captain Ivo Bligh on his next visit to Australia is said to contain the ashes of a set of bails. A replica of this urn forms the 'trophy' in the Ashes contests.

Bails

The bails are the two small shaped pieces of wood that sit across the top of the three stumps to make the wicket which the batsman defends. The bails must be dislodged for the batsman to be declared out.

Beamer

A delivery which is bowled quickly straight at the batsman – without bouncing – often at or near head height.

Bite

The word used to describe the amount of turn a spin bowler can get out of a pitch.

Block

1. The mark made by a batsman when he takes his guard from the umpire to mark his standing position.

2. A defensive stroke which stops a ball that would have hit the stumps.

Block hole

The hole made by the bat when successive batsmen have taken guard in the same place. It is often referred to when a bowler delivers a ball which pitches on a full length. 'Digging the ball out of the block hole' is a desperate last line of defence against the yorker.

Bodyline

The name given to the notorious series of test matches between Australia and England in 1932–1933 in which the English bowlers were instructed to bowl directly at the bodies of the Australian batsmen. It caused a major scandal at the time.

Bouncer
A short-pitched ball that passes the batsman at a height of anything from waist high to about a metre above his head, depending on the speed of the ball and the bounce of the pitch.

Boundary
The perimeter of the playing area, marked in white.

Bump ball
A ball that hits the ground immediately after it has come off the bat and then shoots up into the air to be caught by a fielder. Spectators are often fooled into thinking that the batsman is out, but he isn't.

Bye
A run that is added to the batting team's total but that doesn't come off the bat. Leg byes are runs scored off the pads. Byes are not counted against the bowler.

Cherry (slang)
A new ball, so-called because of its perfect cherry-red colour.

Chin music
A sustained attack of bouncers by a bowling attack. It became associated with the pace bowling of the West Indies in the 1970s and 1980s.

Chinaman
A ball from a left-arm spin bowler that moves off the ground like an off-break, completely contrary to expectations. Named after West Indian spinner EE Achong, a player of Chinese origin, who was a master of the delivery.

Chucking (also throwing)
Bowling the ball with the delivery arm crooked rather than straight. It is against the laws of cricket and will be ruled a no-ball by the umpires.

Corridor of uncertainty

A term coined by the former England cricketer Geoffrey Boycott to describe the ideal area in which to pitch a cricket ball which forces a batsman to play at the ball for fear that it might hit his stumps, but also just wide enough of the stumps to get an edged catch.

Cow corner

An area of the ground (somewhere between long on and deep square leg) that is the ultimate destination of an agricultural cross-batted shot.

Crease

The area that the batsman occupies in front of the wicket.

Cross bat

To play the ball across the line of its trajectory. This is dangerous as it can lead to edged shots.

Dead ball

When the ball has been returned by a fielder to the wicketkeeper or bowler after a delivery (or after runs have been scored) the ball is dead and no runs or wickets may be taken. The batsmen cannot be run out if the ball is dead.

Declaration

A tactical decision made by the captain of the batting side to bring the team's innings to a close, even if there are batsmen still to bat.

Deep

A fielding position in the outfield, close to the boundary.

Dolly

A simple catch.

Doosra

A spin bowler's delivery that is expected to turn the same way as his usual delivery, but that actually turns in the opposite direction. It is a Hindi word meaning 'the other one'.

Drive

An attacking batting stroke, played by the batsman with his leading foot down the wicket towards the bowler.

Duck (Golden Duck)

A duck is a score of 0. A golden duck is a first-ball duck. (See king pair).

Feather

A faint touch from the batsman as the ball passes. Can be almost impossible to hear, and hence to give out if you're an umpire.

Flipper

A wrist spinner's delivery that comes out of the back of the hand and is much flatter and faster in its trajectory as a result.

Follow-on

If the team batting second fail to score enough runs (usually 200 less than the team batting first, but it may be less), they can be asked to follow-on by the opposing captain. They will then have to start their second innings immediately.

Full toss

A delivery that is so full it doesn't touch the pitch, but is on a normal line.

Gardening

The habit of batsmen – sometimes intent on time-wasting – of tapping the wicket on a good length between deliveries to flatten the ground and ensure the ball doesn't hit an uneven patch.

Gate

The space between a batsman's pad and his bat when he plays a defensive shot. When the ball squeezes through this gap and hits the stumps, the batsman is 'bowled through the gate'.

Googly

Like a doosra, a googly is a delivery by a wrist spinner which is bowled to look as if it's going to turn one way, but actually turns the opposite way (see also wrong'un).

Grubber

Another term for a shooter.

Guard

When a batsman begins his innings, he takes guard – a position in line with the stumps marked with a block which enables the batsman to know where he is in relation to the stumps behind him. Batsmen typically take their guard in a line from middle stump, leg stump (the stump nearest their legs) or from a space between the two (middle and leg).

Gully

An off-side fielding position between point – who fields at right angles to the batsman – and the slips – who field behind the wicket. Gully is so-called because it is the corridor or gap between the other positions.

Half volley

A delivery which is slightly short of a good length which often comes to the batsman at the perfect height to hit.

Hat-trick

When a bowler takes three wickets with three successive deliveries, this is described as a hat-trick. There are many suggested definitions of the term, from a hat being awarded to anyone who achieved the feat to a collection being taken in a hat and waged against the likelihood of this great achievement taking place.

Hook

A risky shot, normally played off short, fast bowling, which resembles a baseball shot and is normally played behind the batsman on the leg side. A hook shot can be a good way to score six runs, but as it's played in the air with little control, it's also a good way to get out.

Innings

An innings is the turn of each team to bat. One-day games are single innings matches, games played over two or more days will allow each team two innings.

Jaffa (slang)

An unplayable delivery that leaves the batsman completely confused. This slang originates from Australia and may derive from the popular Australian sweet of the same name – meaning the delivery is 'sweet'.

(King) pair

A pair is a score of 0 (ducks) by a batsman in both innings of a match. A king pair is two first-ball ducks. The word pair is believed to come from 'a pair of spectacles' – representing the two 00s.

Late cut

A very delicate shot in which the batsman waits until the ball has almost gone past him and then gently directs it through the slip or gully area.

Leg before wicket

If a ball is bowled in such a way that it hits (or would hit) the pitch in line with the wickets and would then go on to hit the wicket, but strikes the batsman on the leg or body instead, the umpire may decide the ball would have hit the wicket and will give him out if the fielding side appeal.

Leg cutter

A delivery bowled by a fast or medium-paced bowler which moves towards the batsman's legs when it pitches. This is achieved by 'cutting' the fingers across the seam when releasing the ball, the same way as a spinner would bowl a leg break.

Length

A good length delivery is one that hits the pitch in the perfect place to cause uncertainty in the batsman's mind whether to play forward or back to the ball. A good length may vary depending on the bounce and pace of the wicket. A ball that hits the pitch closer to the batsman is a full length and one that is further from him is a short length delivery.

Line (of delivery)

The right line is the other prerequisite of a good delivery. The ball should be close enough to the stumps to make the batsman play it, for fear it will hit the stumps, and not so far down his leg or off side that he can hit it away without fear of being bowled.

Long hop

A slow and short ball that is easy to score a run from. Beware: lots of batsmen get caught in the **deep** off long hops which they underestimate.

Maiden

A maiden over is one in which no runs are scored that go against the bowler's name in the scorebook (byes don't count against a bowler's name, so a maiden over may be one in which only byes are scored). The word has many possible origins, but is thought to relate either to the perfection of a maiden – the perfect over – or to the purity of a maiden.

Michelle (slang)

A haul of five wickets in an innings – a kind of cricket rhyming slang derived from the surname of the popular US actress Michelle Pfeiffer (five for . . .)

Nelson

A score of 111, believed by superstitious English cricketers to be unlucky as it (falsely) was thought to be connected to Nelson's one arm, one leg and one eye – though Nelson had two legs. The score is also said to resemble a set of stumps without bails – which is very unlucky.

Nightwatchman

A lower order batsman who is brought in towards the end of a day's play when few wickets have fallen to protect the more senior batsmen. His role is to block the ball until the end of play, allowing the more experienced batsmen to stay safely in the pavilion until the conditions are more favourable in the morning.

Non-striker

The batsman who is at the bowler's end in the over is called the non-striker.

Over

A set of six deliveries bowled from one end of the pitch. At the end of each over, the play switches to the opposite end of the pitch and a different bowler begins another over. An extra ball must be bowled in an over for any deliveries that are unlawful (no-ball or wide).

Pie-thrower (slang)

A derogatory term used to describe an inexperienced or unskilful bowler.

Pitch

1. The noun used to describe the 22-yard playing surface in the centre of the ground with stumps at either end. Also called a wicket.

2. A verb used to describe the moment of impact of the ball on the ground after the bowler has released it – ie 'the ball pitched on leg stump, but turned to off stump'.

Plumb

If a batsman is trapped leg before wicket without any doubt that the delivery would have gone on to hit the stumps, he is described as being 'plumb'. This comes from the decorator's plumb line, a piece of lead on string which is used to mark a straight line.

Pull

A cross-batted shot, similar to a hook, but normally with more control, directed along the ground on the leg side.

Rabbit

A rabbit is an inexperienced or unskilful batsman, so-called because he resembles a rabbit caught in the headlights of a car as the bowler comes in to bowl.

Reverse swing

As with a googly, this involves the ball moving in the opposite direction to expectations – ie an away swinger suddenly swinging in to the batsman's legs – but unlike a googly the movement is in the air, not on the ground.

Round the wicket

If a right-handed bowler bowls to a right-handed batsman, he delivers the ball from the left side of the stumps – this is known as 'over the wicket' bowling. If the bowler wants to change the line of his delivery, he can choose to bowl 'round the wicket' from the right side of the stumps.

Runner

A substitute brought on to run in place of a batsman who has an injury and cannot run himself. If a runner is run out, the batsman he 'represents' is run out.

Shooter

A delivery that comes through to the batsman much lower than expected after it pitches.

Sledging

The practice of fielders abusing (sometimes quite mildly, sometimes aggressively) the batsman while he is trying to concentrate.

Snick

A faint edge off the bat. See also feather.

Stance

The position a batsman takes while waiting for the ball. Most batsmen have a side-on stance, so only their left side is visible to the bowler, but some have a face-on stance where they face the bowler fully.

Stand

The number of runs scored by two batsmen together until one of them is out or the innings is closed, is called a stand.

Sticky wicket (slang)

A phrase used to describe a difficult batting surface.

Strike bowler

The leading, or most effective, wicket-taker in a team.

Stumps

The three cylindrical wooden stakes at either end of the pitch which are topped by bails.

Sweep

A cross-batted shot, normally played off slow bowling, where the batsman goes down on one knee and sweeps the ball to the leg side.

Tail

The less able batsmen in a team are known as the tail (or tail-end). Some teams have a long tail of specialist bowlers who are not talented batsmen – from batsmen number eight through to 11. If the tail-enders bat well in an innings and add valuable runs to the team's total the tail is said to 'wag'.

Toe end

The name given to the bottom or base of the bat. When storing a bat over winter it is important to keep the toe end protected as it is often the only untreated section of wood and therefore it is liable to damp penetration.

Track (slang)

Another word for wicket or pitch.

Wicket

1. The stumps and bails at either end of the pitch.

2. An alternative word used to describe the pitch itself.

3. The act of dismissing a batsman is known as 'taking a wicket'.

4. Every time a batsman is dismissed, the number of 'wickets down' is increased in the scorebook and scoreboard, from 0 wickets at the beginning of the innings to 10 wickets (all out) at the end.

Wrong'un

See googly and doosra.

Yorker

A delivery that pitches on a very full length with the intention of getting underneath the batsman's defences if he can't get his bat onto the ground fast enough to prevent the ball squeezing through and hitting his stumps.

CRICKET QUIZ

So you think you know cricket? See how you get on in this quiz:

1. Who scored 333 for England against Pakistan at Lord's in 1990?

2. Who is the only cricketer to make centuries in each of his first three test matches?

3. Who scored a total of just one run in his first six test match innings?

4. Name two cricketers who have played at senior level for two different international teams since 1970.

5. What is the name of the trophy awarded to the winners of England v West Indies test match series?

6. Who is the only test cricketer to be given out for obstructing the field?

7. Who was the first cricket writer to be knighted for services to the game?

8. What was significant about the second day of the Lord's test between England and West Indies in 2000?

9. Which player has won the most Man of the Match awards in one day international cricket?

10. Which player has won the most Man of the Match awards in test match cricket?

11. Who was the youngest player to play in a test match?

12. Who was the oldest player to play in a test match?

13. Five players share the record for most catches (not by a wicket-keeper) in a test match innings – how many catches did they take?

14. Northamptonshire scored the lowest first class innings total in their English country championship game against Gloucestershire in 1907. What was the score?

15. Only four players in test match cricket history have scored 2,000 runs, taken 200 wickets and 100 catches. Name them.

(Answers can be found on p. 174)

Cricket Quiz Answers

1. Graham Gooch.
2. Mohammad Azharrudin of India.
3. Marvan Atapattu of Sri Lanka.
4. John Traicos (South Africa and Zimbabwe) and Kepler Wessels (Australia and South Africa).
5. The Wisden Trophy.
6. Len Hutton of England.
7. Neville Cardus.
8. It was the only time in history that part of all four innings of a test have been played in the same day.
9. Sachin Tendulkar of India.
10. Jacques Kallis of South Africa.
11. Hasan Raza of Pakistan (14 years) in 1996.
12. Wilfred Rhodes of England (52 years) in 1930.
13. Five.
14. 12 all out.
15. Ian Botham, Shane Warne, Jacques Kallis and Gary Sobers.

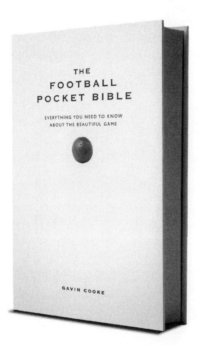

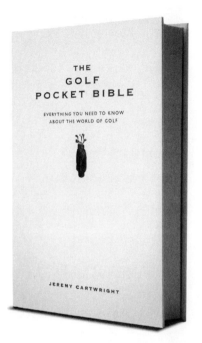